jQuery Mobile

jQuery Mobile

Jon Reid

O'REILLY®

Beijing · Cambridge · Farnham · Köln · Sebastopol · Tokyo

jQuery Mobile
by Jon Reid

Copyright © 2011 Jonathan Reid. All rights reserved.
Printed in the United States of America.

Published by O'Reilly Media, Inc., 1005 Gravenstein Highway North, Sebastopol, CA 95472.

O'Reilly books may be purchased for educational, business, or sales promotional use. Online editions are also available for most titles (*http://my.safaribooksonline.com*). For more information, contact our corporate/institutional sales department: (800) 998-9938 or *corporate@oreilly.com*.

Editor: Mary Treseler	**Cover Designer:** Karen Montgomery
Production Editor: Jasmine Perez	**Interior Designer:** David Futato
Proofreader: Jasmine Perez	**Illustrator:** Robert Romano

Printing History:

June 2011:	First Edition.

ISBN: 978-1-449-30668-7

[LSI]   [2011-08-11]

1313075823

Table of Contents

Preface

Introduction

Mobile applications come in two basic flavors: native applications, which are compiled programs that run natively on the device, and mobile web applications, which run inside a web browser on the device.

Native applications get almost all of the press these days, especially given the financial success of the iTunes App Store and the Android Market. And with good reason, as native applications have many advantages: they are fast, have access to all of the power of the platform they are built for, and so forth. However, native applications suffer from one important limitation: they are not portable. If you want to make your application available on multiple platforms, you either have to write it in multiple languages (resulting in multiple code bases to maintain) or use a platform abstraction layer like Titanium or PhoneGap.

Mobile web applications, on the other hand, are created in HTML, CSS, and JavaScript, and run in the web browser on the mobile device. This means one code base to maintain, but mobile web applications still need to account for variations in web browsers across platforms.

Enter jQuery Mobile. Based on the popular jQuery JavaScript library, jQuery Mobile is designed to create mobile web applications that function on a broad range of devices. With jQuery Mobile, it is possible to quickly create mobile web applications that look and behave consistently across all supported devices, and that have advanced user interface capabilities. jQuery Mobile gives the developer a standard set of layouts, user interface widgets, and interactions, as well as a rich API for applying and extending them.

jQuery Mobile is not yet in production—as of this writing, it is in its Alpha 4 release, with the beta coming soon.

Even so, the library already has a broad set of features and is remarkably stable. In fact, I have already used it in one production project with great success, and if you review posts on the jQuery Mobile forums, you'll see that there are many people using jQuery

Mobile in production. As jQuery Mobile advances, we hope to update this ebook to cover new features and provide new tips and techniques.

What This Book Covers

This book covers how the jQuery Mobile library works, and how to use it to create mobile web applications. While I was writing this book I was engaged in a project in which I was using jQuery Mobile to create a mobile web application. This gave me a unique insight into how to use jQuery Mobile in a production environment, so this book takes a practical approach for using the library and focuses on example code and screenshots. In addition, throughout the book there are "Under The Hood" sections where I explore a topic in more detail: page initialization, using swipe events to trigger page transitions, animation in a jQuery Mobile application, and so forth.

In Chapter 1, we will provide a high-level overview of jQuery Mobile, how it works, and how to use it. If you follow the examples in the chapter, at the end of the chapter you will have built your first jQuery Mobile application. It won't do much, but it will show how easy it is to set up a jQuery Mobile application and introduce you to some important jQuery Mobile concepts.

Chapter 2 covers paging and navigation in jQuery Mobile, including dialogs, AJAX content, and history.

In Chapter 3, we will cover the UI elements that jQuery Mobile can create: toolbars, buttons, lists, form elements, and layout grids.

In Chapter 4, we will cover the jQuery Mobile theme framework, how to use it, and how to customize it.

In Chapter 5, we will take a look at the new events that jQuery Mobile creates, the methods it exposes, and how to customize jQuery Mobile for your own applications.

Chapter 6 is where we will put everything together and build an actual mobile application: jqmTweet. We'll walk through how to approach building a mobile application with jQuery Mobile from start to finish.

What You Need To Know

This book assumes you are already familiar with the jQuery JavaScript library. You should be able to create jQuery selectors and apply jQuery methods to them.

This book assumes you are familiar with HTML markup and Cascading Style Sheets. Throughout the code examples, we will be using HTML 5 and CSS 3, and employing industry best practices like semantic markup and progressive enhancement.

This book also assumes that you have a basic familiarity with mobile web browsers. Though jQuery Mobile aims to provide a cross-platform API, it is still necessary for a mobile web developer to understand mobile browsers and their capabilities.

Finally, this book assumes you are familiar with the technologies of the web: HTTP, clients and servers, security, etc.

Conventions Used In This Book

The following typographical conventions are used in this book:

Italic

Indicates a term, URL, email address, or filenames or extensions.

`Constant Width`

Used for code examples and for code elements such as variable names, function names, keywords, etc. that are included in regular paragraphs.

`Constant width italic`

Shows text that should be replaced with user-supplied values or by values determined by context.

> This signifies a tip, suggestion, or note of interest.

> This indicates a warning or caution: a bug in the library, a common problem, etc.

Using Code Examples

This book is here to help you get your job done. In general, you may use the code in this book in your programs and documentation. You do not need to contact us for permission unless you're reproducing a significant portion of the code. For example, writing a program that uses several chunks of code from this book does not require permission. Selling or distributing a CD-ROM of examples from O'Reilly books does require permission. Answering a question by citing this book and quoting example code does not require permission. Incorporating a significant amount of example code from this book into your product's documentation does require permission.

We appreciate, but do not require, attribution. An attribution usually includes the title, author, publisher, and ISBN. For example: *"jQuery Mobile* by Jon Reid (O'Reilly). Copyright 2011 Jonathan Reid, 978-1-449-30668-7."

If you feel your use of code examples falls outside fair use or the permission given above, feel free to contact us at *permissions@oreilly.com*.

Safari® Books Online

Safari Books Online is an on-demand digital library that lets you easily search over 7,500 technology and creative reference books and videos to find the answers you need quickly.

With a subscription, you can read any page and watch any video from our library online. Read books on your cell phone and mobile devices. Access new titles before they are available for print, and get exclusive access to manuscripts in development and post feedback for the authors. Copy and paste code samples, organize your favorites, download chapters, bookmark key sections, create notes, print out pages, and benefit from tons of other time-saving features.

O'Reilly Media has uploaded this book to the Safari Books Online service. To have full digital access to this book and others on similar topics from O'Reilly and other publishers, sign up for free at *http://my.safaribooksonline.com*.

How to Contact Us

Please address comments and questions concerning this book to the publisher:

O'Reilly Media, Inc.
1005 Gravenstein Highway North
Sebastopol, CA 95472
800-998-9938 (in the United States or Canada)
707-829-0515 (international or local)
707-829-0104 (fax)

We have a web page for this book, where we list errata, examples, and any additional information. You can access this page at:

http://www.oreilly.com/catalog/0636920020585

To comment or ask technical questions about this book, send email to:

bookquestions@oreilly.com

For more information about our books, courses, conferences, and news, see our website at *http://www.oreilly.com*.

Find us on Facebook: *http://facebook.com/oreilly*

Follow us on Twitter: *http://twitter.com/oreillymedia*

Watch us on YouTube: *http://www.youtube.com/oreillymedia*

Acknowledgments

I'd like to thank RJ Owen for volunteering to do the technical review of this book. His honesty and encouragement helped make this book a success.

I also want to thank Juan Sanchez for providing suggestions for the "Under The Hood" sections in the book.

The HTML development team at EffectiveUI patiently listened to me rave about jQuery Mobile and obsess about this book: Aaron Congleton, Ryan McGinty, Kevin Bauman, Shane Church, Tony Walt, and George Robison. Thanks, guys.

CHAPTER 1

Meet jQuery Mobile

jQuery Mobile is a set of jQuery plug-ins and widgets that aim to provide a cross-platform API for creating mobile web applications. In terms of code implementation, jQuery Mobile is very similar to jQuery UI, but while jQuery UI is focused on desktop applications, jQuery Mobile is built with mobile devices in mind.

As of this writing, jQuery Mobile is still in its Alpha 4 release, with beta just around the corner. There are still plenty of issues that are being fixed, but the jQuery Mobile development team has said that they consider the library to be feature-complete for their 1.0 release. Although the documentation is sparse, especially compared to the extensive documentation for the jQuery project itself, the forums are very active (*http://forum.jquery.com/jquery-mobile*).

Even so, many people are already using jQuery Mobile in production, which is a testament not only to the stability and quality of the library, but of how easy it is to use.

Overview of the jQuery Mobile Library

As of this writing, jQuery Mobile consists of four files: a JavaScript file, a CSS file, and two PNG graphic sprites.

The JavaScript file is meant to be loaded after the base jQuery library. This script file performs various tasks, like creating widgets, applying event listeners, and enabling the API.

jQuery Mobile also includes a Cascading Style Sheet which specifies layout and appearance of jQuery Mobile page elements. The Style Sheet also specifies transitions and animations with CSS3 transforms.

Finally, jQuery Mobile includes a small set of graphics for user interface elements. These are simple, standardized icons for navigation.

You can download the entire jQuery Mobile package (the JavaScript library, the CSS, and the graphics) or you can access them through the project's CDN. See the jQuery

Mobile project download page for specifics. (*http://jquerymobile.com/download/*) In the examples for this book, we will be using the CDN.

How jQuery Mobile Works

jQuery Mobile uses HTML 5 and CSS 3 features to enhance basic HTML markup to create a consistent mobile experience across supported platforms. jQuery Mobile makes heavy use of the HTML 5 specification for custom `data-` attributes (available for review at *http://dev.w3.org/html5/spec/elements.html#embedding-custom-non-visible-data-with-the-data-attributes*). Using this method, it is possible to embed data into valid HTML 5 markup. jQuery Mobile has a large vocabulary of `data-` attributes.

Upon initialization, jQuery Mobile selects elements based on their `data-` attributes and enhances them by inserting extra markup, adding new CSS classes, and applying event handlers. This enables you to quickly write basic semantic markup and leave it to jQuery Mobile to transform your simple markup into complex user interface elements.

 It's actually an interesting exercise to see what jQuery Mobile adds to your basic markup. To do this, you will need the ability to view source both before and after JavaScript has been applied to a page—in most browsers, the "view source" menu option will only show you the unenhanced source. However, most browsers have "view generated source" plug-ins available, and the ability to view generated source is built into some browser-based web development toolbars.

Create Your First jQuery Mobile Application

The best way to understand jQuery Mobile is to dive right in. Begin by creating a simple HTML 5 page that includes the jQuery and jQuery Mobile libraries, as shown in Example 1-1.

Example 1-1. Basic HTML5 page for a jQuery Mobile application

```
<!DOCTYPE html>
<html>
  <head>
    <title>jQuery Mobile Application</title>
    <link rel="stylesheet" href="http://code.jquery.com/mobile/1.0a4.1/
      jquery.mobile-1.0a4.1.min.css" />
    <script src="http://code.jquery.com/jquery-1.5.2.min.js"></script>
    <script src="http://code.jquery.com/mobile/1.0a4.1/jquery.mobile-1.0a4.1.min.js">
  </script>
  </head>
  <body>
  </body>
</html>
```

This includes everything you need to start building a jQuery Mobile application.

Next, we need to include some content. Content should be marked up semantically, and since we're using HTML 5, we have access to all of the new tags like `header`, `footer`, `section`, `nav`, etc. We can mark up our content using those tags, or we simply block off our content using `div` tags.

For our first example, we want to create a page in our application that is a self-contained section, with a header, content area, and footer. (We'll discuss the details of pages and views in jQuery Mobile in the next chapter. For now, we'll just focus on the simplest case.) Using div-based markup, we would create something like what is shown in Example 1-2.

Example 1-2. Old and busted: div-based markup

```
<div class="section" id="page1">
  <div class="header"><h1>jQuery Mobile</h1></div>
  <div class="content">
    <p>First page!</p>
  </div>
  <div class="footer"><h1>O'Reilly</h1></div>
</div>
```

Or we can mark up the same content using the HTML 5 tags `section`, `header`, and `footer`, as shown in Example 1-3.

Example 1-3. New hotness: HTML 5 markup

```
<section id="page1">
  <header><h1>jQuery Mobile</h1></header>
  <div class="content">
    <p>First page!</p>
  </div>
  <footer><h1>O'Reilly</h1></footer>
</section>
```

jQuery Mobile will work with either markup style, though as we move forward in this book, we will use the HTML 5 markup.

jQuery Mobile doesn't need specific markup, but it does need us to indicate the roles of the content areas somehow. To do this, jQuery Mobile uses a custom `data-` attribute: `data-role`. Valid `data-role` values include `page`, `header`, `content`, and `footer`.

This is our first encounter with a custom `data-` attribute. jQuery Mobile uses them extensively to designate functionality, layout, and behaviors. We'll learn more about them in later chapters, so for right now we'll just focus on the `data-role` attribute.

Applying the appropriate `data-role` attributes, our HTML 5 markup would be written as shown in Example 1-4.

Example 1-4. jQuery Mobile data-role attributes applied to HTML 5 markup

```
<section id="page1" data-role="page">
  <header data-role="header"><h1>jQuery Mobile</h1></header>
  <div class="content" data-role="content">
    <p>First page!</p>
  </div>
  <footer data-role="footer"><h1>O'Reilly</h1></footer>
</section>
```

That is all you need to do to create an application in jQuery Mobile. It will do all the rest for you.

To view your new web application, you can run it locally in an HTML 5 capable browser (such as Safari), as shown in Figure 1-1.

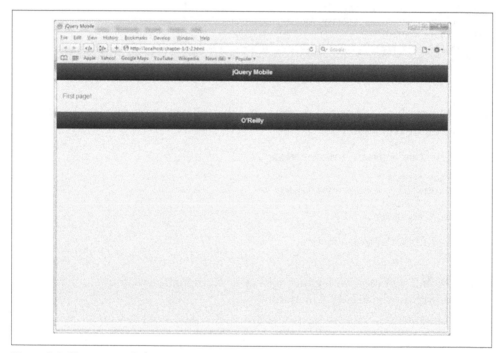

Figure 1-1. First page in Safari

This will give you an idea of what it will look like and how it will perform, but to really test the application you will need to view it in a mobile device.

You can use various emulators that come with the platform application development SDKs, but the ideal way to test the application is to serve it via a web server and use a mobile device to browse it. This will give you the best feel for how the application behaves.

Setting yourself up to serve your content locally is actually quite easy. My favorite drop-in tool is XAMPP, available at *http://www.apache friends.org/en/xampp.html*. It is available for Windows, OS X, Linux, and Solaris, and has great step-by-step tutorials and how-to guides.

Throughout this book, we will be using screen shots from an iPhone, and our current application is shown in Figure 1-2.

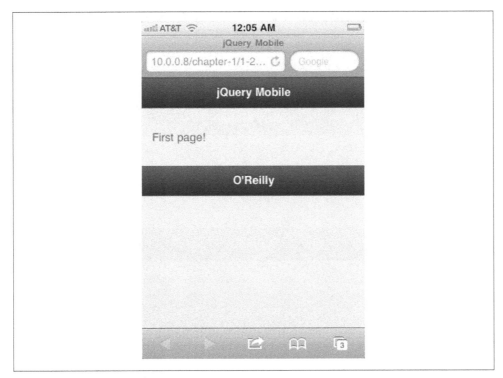

Figure 1-2. First page in iPhone

Adding another page is a simple matter of copying and pasting our code and changing the `id` of the containing `section` and updating the content to reflect a new page, as shown in Example 1-5.

Example 1-5. Adding a second page to the sample application

```
<section id="page2" data-role="page">
  <header data-role="header"><h1>jQuery Mobile</h1></header>
  <div class="content" data-role="content">
    <p>Second page!</p>
  </div>
  <footer data-role="footer"><h1>O'Reilly</h1></footer>
</section>
```

Navigation between pages is simple: just add a link to your content area in the first page of the application, as shown in Example 1-6.

Example 1-6. Adding a link to second page

```
<div class="content" data-role="content">
  <p>First page!</p>
  <p><a href="#page2">Go to the second page!</a></p>
</div>
```

Now when you refresh the application, you will see a link to tap, as shown in Figure 1-3.

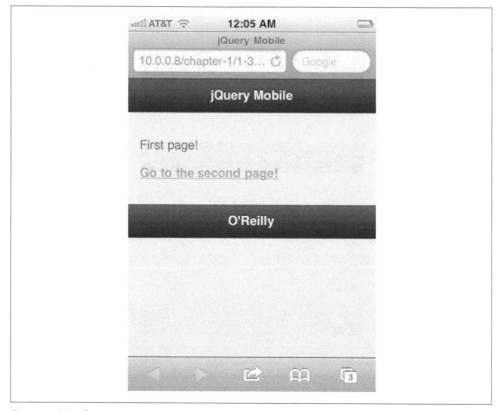

Figure 1-3. Link to next page

Tapping the link will transition to the next screen. jQuery Mobile will automatically handle the page transition animation, and will automatically provide a back button in the header.

Tapping on the back button will return you to the previous page, and again jQuery Mobile will automatically handle the page transition.

There you have it, your first jQuery Mobile application. It doesn't do much, but it should give you some insight into the simplicity of the framework. All you have to do is mark up your content semantically and then designate roles, functionality, and interactions using custom `data-` attributes. Then sit back and allow jQuery Mobile to do all the work for you.

Under The Hood: the jqmData() Custom Selector

jQuery Mobile has a new custom selector that it uses to select elements with `data-` attributes. You're probably already familiar with jQuery's other built in custom selectors, which include `:has()`, `:contains()`, `:eq()`, etc. These selectors can be used either to directly select elements (e.g. `$("div:contains('foo')")`) or they can be used to filter other selectors (e.g. `$("div").contains('foo')`).

You can select all elements with a `data-role="page"` attribute using the standard jQuery selector `$("[data-role='page']")`. This works fine, but since jQuery Mobile relies so heavily on custom `data-` attributes, it made sense to build a custom selector: `jqmData()`.

To use `jqmData()` to select all elements with a `data-role="page"`, you would use `$(":jqmData(role='page')")`. To select all elements with any custom `data-` attribute within those selected pages, you could use `$(":jqmData(role='page')").jqmData(role)`.

The `jqmData()` selector also automatically handles namespacing. Since jQuery Mobile relies so heavily on data attributes, you should be able to apply a namespace to them to avoid conflicts with other data attributes that won't be used by jQuery Mobile. (For example, instead of `data-role="page"`, it could use `data-`*namespace*`-role="page"` where *namespace-* is a configurable string.) By default, jQuery Mobile does not apply a namespace, but it can be configured to do so using the `$.mobile.ns` configuration option (see "Configuring jQuery Mobile" on page 88 in Chapter 5 for more information). If you do configure a namespace, the `jqmData()` selector will automatically account for it. There was an interesting discussion around adding the namespacing feature to jQuery Mobile, which you can read over on the project's GitHub at *https://github.com/jquery/ jquery-mobile/issues/196*.

CHAPTER 2

Application Structure and Navigation

Pages

As we saw in our first example, jQuery Mobile designates pages using the `data-role` attribute. Behind the scenes, jQuery Mobile selects elements based on this attribute and progressively enhances them, adding CSS classes, any needed markup, and event management. This may seem like a complicated way of handling things—why not simply have regular pages linked like you ordinarily would?—but this methodology gives jQuery Mobile several important features:

Page Transitions

> By handling pages as separate content areas in one document, jQuery Mobile can create smooth page transitions, resulting in an overall "application-like" look and feel.

Navigation Management

> jQuery Mobile can automatically handle page navigation, providing features like back buttons and deep linking.

Efficiency

> Since resources are all contained in one file, the browser does not have to access the network over and over again, as it would with smaller individual files. This will help mitigate application slowness and battery drain on the mobile device. The trade-off is that for a large application there could be an appreciable download time for a large HTML page with many individual jQuery Mobile page views. However, once the file is downloaded and ready, the behavior will be much faster and will not necessarily be dependent on network access.

Internal Pages

As we have already seen, we can mark discrete sections of content as pages within the application with the `data-role="page"`. These sections must be top-level siblings in the document body; it is not possible to nest pages within one another. As shown in Example 2-1, a single HTML document can have as many of these pages as desired.

Example 2-1. Multiple internal pages in one HTML document

```html
<!-- begin first page -->
<section id="page1" data-role="page">
  <header data-role="header"><h1>jQuery Mobile</h1></header>
  <div  data-role="content" class="content">
    <p>First page!</p>
    <p><a href="#page2">Go to Second Page</a></p>
  </div>
  <footer data-role="footer"><h1>O'Reilly</h1></footer>
</section>
<!-- end first page -->

<!-- Begin second page -->
<section id="page2" data-role="page">
  <header data-role="header"><h1>jQuery Mobile</h1></header>
  <div data-role="content" class="content">
    <p>Second page!</p>
    <p><a href="#page3">Go to Third Page</a></p>
  </div>
  <footer data-role="footer"><h1>O'Reilly</h1></footer>
</section>
<!-- end second page -->

<!-- begin third page -->
<section id="page3" data-role="page">
  <header data-role="header"><h1>jQuery Mobile</h1></header>
  <div data-role="content" class="content">
    <p>Third page!</p>
    <p><a href="#page1">Go back to First Page</a></p>
  </div>
  <footer data-role="footer"><h1>O'Reilly</h1></footer>
</section>
<!-- end third page -->
```

jQuery Mobile will automatically handle page transitions, back buttons, etc., as the user clicks through the resulting pages of the application (see Figures 2-1, 2-2, and 2-3).

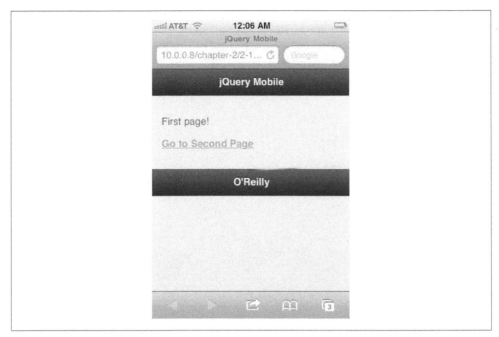

Figure 2-1. Multiple pages (page 1)

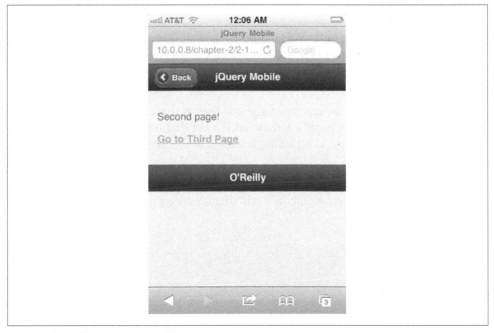

Figure 2-2. Multiple pages (page 2)

Figure 2-3. Multiple pages (page 3)

External Pages

jQuery Mobile will also handle external pages as well. If you link to a separate page instead of to an ID of a `data-role="page"` element within the current document, jQuery Mobile will perform an asynchronous fetch of the requested page and integrate it into the current document, allowing it to perform its page management functions.

jQuery Mobile will fetch the external page and search through it for the first element marked with a `data-role="page"` attribute and insert that into the DOM of the origin document. Any other content, including subsequent elements with `data-role="page"` attributes, will be ignored.

If jQuery Mobile fails to retrieve the page, or if it retrieves the page but fails to find a `data-role="page"` designated element, it will display an error message.

To add an external page to our previous example code, create a file called "external.html" and include the markup shown in Example 2-2.

Example 2-2. External.html

```
<!DOCTYPE html>
<html>
  <head>
    <meta charset="utf-8" />
  </head>
  <body>

    <p>This content will be ignored.</p>

    <!-- Begin Page 4 -->
    <section id="page4" data-role="page">
      <header data-role="header"><h1>jQuery Mobile</h1></header>
      <div class="content" data-role="content">
        <p>External Page!</p>
        <p><a href="#page1">Go to First Page</a>.</p>
      </div>
      <footer data-role="footer"><h1>O'Reilly</h1></footer>
    </section>
    <!-- End Page 4-->

    <h3>This content will be ignored as well.</h3>

  </body>
</html>
```

To load the new page, simply add a link to it in the markup for the third page of our application:

```
    <!-- begin third page -->
    <section id="page3" data-role="page">
      <header data-role="header"><h1>jQuery Mobile</h1></header>
      <div data-role="content" class="content">
        <p>Third page!</p>
        <p><a href="external.html">Go to external page</a></p>
      </div>
      <footer data-role="footer"><h1>O'Reilly</h1></footer>
    </section>
    <!-- end third page -->
```

This will produce the screen shown in Figure 2-4 on the third page of our application.

Figure 2-4. Link to external page

And when we tap the "Go to external page" link, jQuery Mobile will display the loading dialog and attempt to fetch and insert the external.html page. If it succeeds, it will display the page shown in Figure 2-5.

And it now becomes a part of the application and can be accessed from any other page as if it were included in the original DOM.

 When creating pages that will be loaded asynchronously, make sure you do not introduce duplicate IDs into the original DOM.

Overriding Asynchronous Page Fetching

Sometimes you will want to actually load a page normally, rather than having jQuery Mobile fetch it asynchronously and integrate it into the current DOM. You can override the AJAX loading in two ways: specifying a `target` attribute on a link (such as `"_blank"`) or by specifying a `rel="external"` attribute on the link.

Figure 2-5. External page

Under The Hood: Page Initialization in jQuery Mobile

As jQuery Mobile initializes, it runs through the following steps:

1. Triggers the `beforecreate` event (see "Initialization Events" on page 83 in Chapter 5 for more information)
2. Adds the `ui-page` class to all page elements
3. Adds the `ui-nojs` class to all page elements that had `data-role="none"` or `data-role="nojs"` applied to them
4. Looks for child elements that have a `data-` attribute and:
   a. Adds theming classes
   b. Adds appropriate ARIA `role` and `aria-level` attributes
   c. Adds a back button to the header (if there isn't one already in the markup) for pages beyond the first
5. Then it enhances form controls, buttons, and control groups (see Chapter 3 for more information on these individual elements)
6. Finally, it fixes toolbars as specified (see "Positioning the Header and Footer" on page 43 in Chapter 3 for details)

All of these enhancements are done within the page widget, and it transforms the original markup shown in Example 2-3 into the enhanced markup shown in Example 2-4.

Example 2-3. Page markup before jQuery Mobile initialization

```
<!-- begin first page -->
<section id="page1" data-role="page">
  <header data-role="header"><h1>jQuery Mobile</h1></header>
  <div  data-role="content">
    <p>First page!</p>
  </div>
  <footer data-role="footer"><h1>O'Reilly</h1></footer>
</section>
<!-- end first page -->
```

Example 2-4. Page markup after jQuery Mobile initialization

```
<!-- begin first page -->
<section class="ui-page ui-body-c ui-page-active"
         data-url="page1"
         id="page1"
         data-role="page">
  <header role="banner"
          class="ui-bar-a ui-header"
          data-role="header">
    <h1 aria-level="1"
        role="heading"
        tabindex="0"
        class="ui-title">Header</h1>
  </header>
  <div role="main" data-role="content" class="ui-content">
    <p>First page!</p>
  </div>
  <footer role="contentinfo"
          class="ui-bar-a ui-footer"
          data-role="footer">
    <h1 aria-level="1"
        role="heading"
        tabindex="0"
        class="ui-title">Footer</h1>
  </footer>
</section>
<!-- end first page -->
```

Notice that the semantics of the markup hasn't changed, all that happened was the addition of ARIA attributes and CSS classes. Other more complex interface elements (like list views) are more heavily enhanced, and jQuery Mobile will even modify markup, usually by adding span or div tags.

It's often useful to examine the alterations jQuery Mobile makes to your markup. Unfortunately, most browsers limit their source view capabilities to just showing the markup that was downloaded from the server, without any changes that might have been made subsequently by JavaScript. Fortunately, most browsers have "view generated source" plug-ins or extensions. Firebug for Firefox, for example, has a view generated source capability, and there are similar extensions for Safari.

Page Hide and Show Events

Because of its asynchronous nature, jQuery Mobile makes the distinction between page load events and page show and hide events. Page load events happen when a file is loaded into the browser in a standard synchronous way. When a file is loaded like this, the usual `jQuery(document).ready()` method is available for use, and jQuery Mobile also fires off other initialization events as well (these will be covered in Chapter 4).

As we have seen, a single HTML file may contain multiple jQuery Mobile page views, and the user can transition between those page views multiple times. These transitions do not fire off the page load events, instead jQuery Mobile provides a set of events that happen every time a page transition occurs. Each of these events provides references to the *event* and *ui* objects:

pagebeforehide

> This event fires on the page being transitioned from, before the transition starts. `ui.nextPage` will be either the page being transitioned to, or an empty jQuery object if there is none.

pagebeforeshow

> This event fires on the page being transitioned to, before the transition starts. `ui.prevPage` will be the page being transitioned from, or an empty jQuery object if there is none.

pagehide

> This event fires on the page being transitioned from, after the transition finishes. `ui.nextPage` will be the jQuery object of the page being transitioned to, or empty if it does not exist.

pageshow

> This event fires on the page being transitioned to, after the transition finishes. `ui.prevPage` will contain the jQuery object of the page being transitioned from, or empty if it does not exist.

These four events provide useful analogs to the `jQuery(document).ready()` call for application page views.

To use these events, you attach event listeners to the appropriate page using `jQuery.bind()`, `jQuery.live()`, or `jQuery.delegate()`.

 jQuery.bind(), jQuery.live(), and jQuery.delegate() are the different methods that jQuery has for binding handlers to event listeners. For more details, consult the jQuery documentation. Here we are using jQuery.bind():

```
<script>
$("#page1").bind("pagehide", function(event, ui) {
  var strAlert = "";
  for (var thing in event) {
    strAlert += thing + " : " + event[thing] + "\n";
```

```
        }
        alert(strAlert);
    });
    </script>
```

For pages that are all contained within the same document, `jQuery.bind()` is sufficient. For pages that will be asynchronously loaded by jQuery Mobile, use `jQuery.dele` `gate()` or `jQuery.live()`.

 When building a jQuery application, it is common practice to bind your event handlers on document load. You can do something similar using jQuery Mobile's page hide and show events, but be careful. Since the page hide and show events are triggered every time a page transition happens, you might bind the event handlers more than once. For example, if you bind a click event listener to an element within a page show event, that click event listener will be bound every time that page is shown. If you are only using that page once, that's fine, but if the user goes to that page multiple times, then the event listener will be bound multiple times.

To get around this problem, you can either check to see if you have already bound the event handler (and if you have, do not bind it again), or clear the binding each time before you rebind. If you use the latter method, namespacing your bindings can be particularly useful. For more information on namespaced events, see *http://docs.jquery.com/ Namespaced_Events*. Namespaced events is a useful tool to have in your jQuery toolbox.

Under The Hood: A jQuery Mobile Page Initialization Pattern

Consider the markup shown in Example 2-5 for a set of mobile application pages.

Example 2-5. jqmTwit

```html
<!-- begin first page -->
<section id="page1" data-role="page">
  <header data-role="header">
      <h1>jqmTwit</h1>
  </header>
  <div  data-role="content" class="content">
    <p>Twitter feed goes here.</p>
    <p><a href="#page2">Settings</a></p>
  </div>
  <footer data-role="footer">
      <h2>Because the world needed another Twitter app.</h2>
  </footer>
</section>
<!-- end first page -->

<!-- Begin second page -->
<section id="page2" data-role="page">
```

```
<header data-role="header">
    <h1>jqmTwit: Settings</h1>
</header>
<div  data-role="content" class="content">
  <p>Settings go here.</p>
</div>
<footer data-role="footer">
    <h2>Because the world needed another Twitter app.</h2>
</footer>
</section>
<!-- end second page -->
```

When the user first fires up the app, you'll need to fill in the twitter feed. If the user goes to the settings page, you'll need to refresh the twitter feed when they return to the main page. So you'd end up with some JavaScript, as shown in Example 2-6 .

Example 2-6. jqmTwit initialization script

```
<script>
$(document).ready(function() {

    // Refresh the feed on first load
    // (pretend we've written this function elsewhere)
    refreshFeed();

    $("#page1").bind("pageshow", function(event, ui) {
        // Refresh the feed on subsequent page shows
        refreshFeed();
    })
})
</script>
```

This is a very simple example and is missing a lot of detail, but it does show the beginnings of a useful jQuery Mobile page initialization pattern:

1. Upon document ready, initialize anything that needs to happen on the first page, plus any event listeners for elements throughout the application

2. Bind pageshow and pagehide events to pages as needed to handle transitions to and from them.

This simple pattern works well and is extensible for complicated applications. It's also easy to wrap in the jQuery plug-in pattern (see "Under The Hood: Using Swipe Events to Trigger Page Transitions" on page 81 in Chapter 5 for a full example of using the jQuery plug-in pattern to create an application initialization plug-in). The only thing to watch out for is to make sure your application can handle it if the user hits the refresh button. The easiest way to do this is to make sure that the initialization events that fire on document ready make sure that an expected view is being shown in an expected state.

Dialogs

Any valid jQuery Mobile page can also be displayed as a dialog by simply adding the `data-rel="dialog"` attribute to the link, as shown in Example 2-7. This signals jQuery Mobile to add extra styles to the page when it is displayed, such as rounded corners, margins, and drop shadows, so that it appears to be hovering over the rest of the application.

Example 2-7. Calling a dialog

```
<!-- begin first page -->
<section id="page1" data-role="page">
  <header data-role="header"><h1>jQuery Mobile</h1></header>
  <div  data-role="content" class="content">
    <p>First page!</p>
    <p><a href="#page2" data-rel="dialog">Open page 2 as a dialog</a></p>
  </div>
  <footer data-role="footer"><h1>O'Reilly</h1></footer>
</section>
<!-- end first page -->

<!-- Begin second page -->
<section id="page2" data-role="page">
  <header data-role="header"><h1>jQuery Mobile</h1></header>
  <div data-role="content" class="content">
    <p>Second page!</p>
  </div>
  <footer data-role="footer"><h1>O'Reilly</h1></footer>
</section>
<!-- end second page -->
```

Tapping on this link will result in page 2 being displayed as a modal dialog, as shown in Figure 2-6.

Navigation and History

jQuery Mobile automatically manages the URLs of the various pages and dialogs in the application. Each page (that is to say, each element that has a `data-role="page"` attribute) will have its own unique URL within the application, allowing for bookmarking and deep linking into your application. The URL for each page is stored in the `data-url` attribute which jQuery Mobile attaches to each page's containing element.

As the user moves through the application by tapping on links and buttons, jQuery Mobile updates the `location.hash` object, allowing the framework to use the browser's native history capabilities to store the navigation information.

Figure 2-6. Page 2 as a dialog

 Due to their modal nature, dialogs are not included in the history hash.

As a result, when you need to manually move from page to page in the application, you will need to use jQuery Mobile's changePage() method, so that the framework can correctly handle everything:

changePage(*to* , *transition* , *back* , *changeHash*)

- *to*: one of the following:
  - —a simple string denoting either an element ID or a filename
  - —an array of two elements, with the first being a simple string denoting the element ID or filename of the page to transition from, and the second being a simple string denoting the page to transition to
  - —an object with the following properties:
    - —*url*: the url string of the desired page
    - —*type*: the HTTP verb ("GET" or "POST")
    - —*data*: serialized parameters to send to the url
- *transition*: the name of the desired transition

- *back*: a Boolean indicating whether or not the transition should be in reverse
- *changeHash*: a Boolean indicating whether or not the `location.hash` should be updated upon successful transition

changePage gives you direct access to the framework's page management system so that you can perform more complex event-based paging, as shown in Example 2-8.

Example 2-8. Example uses of changePage

```
<script>
// Go to #page2 when .back-button is clicked, show animation in reverse,
// and do not update the location hash.
$(".back-button").bind("click", function() {
  changePage("#page2", "flip", true, false);
});

// using changePage to submit a form
$("#my-form").bind("submit", function() {
  if (validateFormData()) {
    changePage({
      url: "form-processor.php",
      type: "post",
      data: myFormData
    }, false);
  }
});
</script>
```

Transitions

jQuery Mobile has several animated transitions that can be used when changing pages or displaying dialogs. These transitions are created using CSS 3 transforms, and so are only available on browsers that support that feature.

To specify a transition, apply the `data-transition` property to the link, as shown in Example 2-9. Valid values are:

fade: simply fade the page or dialog in over the previous content

flip: an animated page flip, rotating the current view out with the other view on the reverse side

pop: the page springs into view from the center of the screen

slide: slide in from the left or right, pushing previous content out of the way

slidedown: slide down from the top, over the top of the current content

slideup: slide up to the top, revealing the next content below

Example 2-9. Specifying a transition for a dialog

```
<!-- begin first page -->
<section id="page1" data-role="page">
  <header data-role="header"><h1>jQuery Mobile</h1></header>
  <div  data-role="content" class="content">
    <p>First page!</p>
    <p><a href="#page2"
          data-rel="dialog"
          data-transition="slidedown">Open page 2 as a dialog</a></p>
  </div>
  <footer data-role="footer"><h1>O'Reilly</h1></footer>
</section>
<!-- end first page -->
```

As shown in Example 2-10, each transition can be reversed by specifying the `data-direction="reverse"` property, though this is more useful for some transitions (*slide* and *flip*, for example) than others (*fade* and *pop*, for example). jQuery Mobile will try to employ the reverse transition in certain cases, such as when using the automatic back button, or when hiding a dialog.

Example 2-10. Specifying reverse transitions

```
<!-- begin first page -->
<section id="page1" data-role="page">
  <header data-role="header"><h1>jQuery Mobile</h1></header>
  <div  data-role="content" class="content">
    <p>First page!</p>
    <p><a href="#page2" data-transition="flip">Flip to Page 2</a></p>
  </div>
  <footer data-role="footer"><h1>O'Reilly</h1></footer>
</section>
<!-- end first page -->

<!-- Begin second page -->
<section id="page2" data-role="page">
  <header data-role="header"><h1>jQuery Mobile</h1></header>
  <div data-role="content" class="content">
    <p>Second page!</p>
    <p><a href="#page1" data-transition="flip" data-direction="reverse">Flip back to Page 1</a></p>
  </div>
  <footer data-role="footer"><h1>O'Reilly</h1></footer>
</section>
<!-- end second page -->
```

Under The Hood: Animations in a jQuery Mobile Application

jQuery Mobile makes use of CSS 3 transforms for animating the page transitions. As of this writing, jQuery Mobile uses webkit transforms, so they only work in webkit-based browsers. The good news is that webkit browsers use hardware acceleration to produce CSS animation, so the animations look smooth even on mobile devices.

The transitions are defined as rules within the jQuery Mobile style sheet, and you can use them directly if you wish to animate elements in your application beyond the page transitions that jQuery Mobile provides. It's a simple matter of toggling CSS classes, as shown in Example 2-11.

Example 2-11. Animations in jQuery Mobile

```
<!-- begin first page -->
<section id="page1" data-role="page">
  <header data-role="header">
      <h1>CSS 3 Animations</h1>
  </header>
  <div  data-role="content" class="content">
      <p class="show-menu">Show/Hide Menu</p>
    <div class="sliding-menu slide out">Menu</div>
  </div>
  <footer data-role="footer">
      <h2>jQuery Mobile</h2>
  </footer>
</section>
<!-- end first page -->

<script>
$(document).ready(function() {
  $(".show-menu").click(function() {
    $(".sliding-menu").toggleClass("reverse out in");
  })
})
</script>
```

When you click on the Show/Hide Menu paragraph, the menu element will be animated onto or off of the screen.

There are seven CSS classes that define base animations: `slide`, `slideup`, `slidedown`, `spin`, `fade`, `flip`, and `pop`. In concert with these are the styles `reverse`, `in`, and `out`. By combining these styles, you can animate elements in your application. You'll need to experiment to get the desired effects.

One word of warning: animations are nifty, but they can negatively impact usability and accessibility. Use them judiciously.

CHAPTER 3

Page Elements

Like jQuery UI, jQuery Mobile has many different UI elements. Many of these are based on common mobile UI elements, and are created in the standard jQuery Mobile way: you write semantic markup and then apply a data attribute to the element, and jQuery Mobile enhances the element upon initialization.

Under The Hood: jQuery Plug-ins and Widgets

jQuery Mobile makes extensive use of two standard jQuery development patterns: the plug-in and the widget.

The jQuery plug-in pattern is a way of extending jQuery itself, enabling you to add custom methods. You can then call your custom method just like you would any other jQuery method. The jQuery plug-in pattern is discussed in detail in the jQuery documentation. If you're not familiar with the jQuery plug-in pattern, I highly recommend you read about it and adopt it whenever it is appropriate. I use the jQuery plug-in pattern on a daily basis in my development tasks, and in the context of a jQuery Mobile application, it provides a handy way of encapsulating application and page initialization functions and data managers.

The jQuery widget pattern is slightly more complicated than the jQuery plug-in pattern, but it is also more powerful. A jQuery widget is created using the `jQuery.widget` factory, and like a plug-in, it results in a jQuery method that can be called on any selector. One of the main benefits of using the widget factory is that it can maintain state even after the resulting method is done executing, and the factory will enable garbage collection to avoid memory leaks in browsers.

For example, consider the jQuery UI Accordion widget, which is a favorite of mine. To create an accordion, you write your markup and then apply the `jQuery.accordion()` method to it. During the initialization process, the accordion widget enhances the markup, creates events that you can bind to, and exposes methods you can use to interact with and modify the resulting accordion.

Sound familiar? It should, that's exactly what jQuery Mobile does. Many of the page elements we are about to explore are created as jQuery widgets, and you handle them in exactly the same way.

List Views

jQuery Mobile can produce visually formatted lists that are very similar to the styles seen in native applications.

Basic List View

jQuery Mobile can enhance either an ordered or unordered list. Just apply the `data-role="listview"` to a list, and jQuery Mobile will do the rest (Example 3-1, Figure 3-1).

Example 3-1. Basic list view

```
<h3>Unordered List</h3>
<ul data-role="listview">
  <li>Item</li>
  <li>Item</li>
  <li>Item</li>
</ul>
<h3>Ordered List</h3>
<ol data-role="listview">
  <li>Item</li>
  <li>Item</li>
  <li>Item</li>
</ol>
```

List View Buttons

By default, list view elements have no interactive properties: tapping or swiping on them has no effect. A common use of list views in mobile user interfaces is to have the list items be tappable buttons. To do this with jQuery Mobile, you have to include anchor tags in the list item markup (Example 3-2).

Example 3-2. List view with buttons

```
<h3>Unordered List</h3>
<ul data-role="listview">
  <li><a href="#">Item</a></li>
  <li><a href="#">Item</a></li>
  <li><a href="#">Item</a></li>
</ul>
<h3>Ordered List</h3>
<ol data-role="listview">
  <li><a href="#">Item</a></li>
  <li><a href="#">Item</a></li>
  <li><a href="#">Item</a></li>
</ol>
```

The list items are now tappable (see Figure 3-2). (In this example, of course, these items don't go anywhere; keep reading for a more fully functional example.)

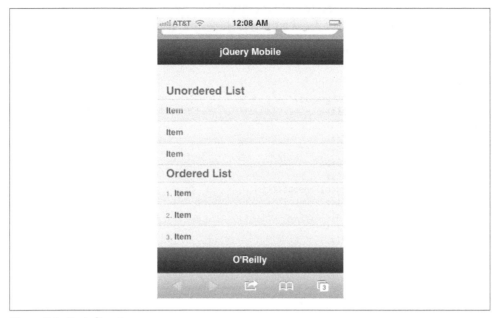

Figure 3-1. Basic list view

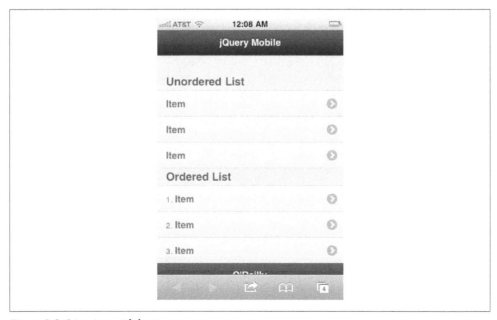

Figure 3-2. List view with buttons

List View Dividers

It's very common to want to have your lists divided by section headers. To do this with jQuery Moble, apply the `data-role="list-divider"` to any list item you want to be a divider, as shown in Example 3-3. Figure 3-3 shows the result.

Example 3-3. List view with dividers

```
<h3>Unordered List</h3>
<ul data-role="listview">
  <li data-role="divider">Things</li>
  <li><a href="#">Item</a></li>
  <li><a href="#">Item</a></li>
  <li><a href="#">Item</a></li>
  <li data-role="divider">Stuff</li>
  <li><a href="#">Item</a></li>
  <li><a href="#">Item</a></li>
  <li data-role="divider">Miscellaneous</li>
  <li><a href="#">Item</a></li>
  <li><a href="#">Item</a></li>
  <li><a href="#">Item</a></li>
  <li><a href="#">Item</a></li>
  <li><a href="#">Item</a></li>
</ul>
<h3>Ordered List</h3>
<ol data-role="listview">
  <li data-role="divider">Group</li>
  <li><a href="#">Item</a></li>
  <li><a href="#">Item</a></li>
  <li><a href="#">Item</a></li>
  <li data-role="divider">Group</li>
  <li><a href="#">Item</a></li>
  <li><a href="#">Item</a></li>
  <li data-role="divider">Group</li>
  <li><a href="#">Item</a></li>
  <li><a href="#">Item</a></li>
  <li><a href="#">Item</a></li>
  <li><a href="#">Item</a></li>
  <li><a href="#">Item</a></li>
</ol>
```

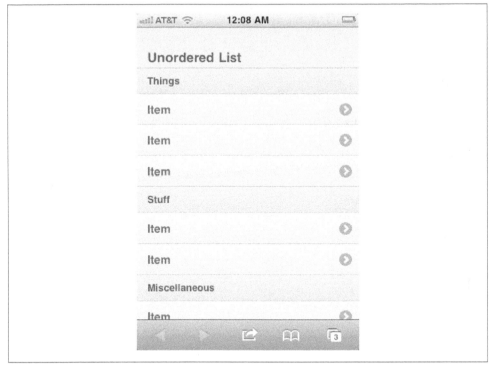

Figure 3-3. List view with dividers

Advanced List Views

Because list views are used widely in mobile user interfaces, jQuery Mobile can produce several of the common variations with just a little more markup.

Nested Lists

jQuery Mobile will take nested lists and produce interactive views into which the user can drill down by tapping on individual items. The first view will consist of the items in the top-level list, and tapping on one of those items will display its sub-list, and so forth. The code for this is shown in Example 3-4; the resulting linked list views are shown in Figures 3-4, 3-5, and 3-6. jQuery Mobile will automatically provide a back button and manage the URL mapping and transitions from page to page.

Example 3-4. Nested list views

```
<h3>Nested List Example</h3>
<ul data-role="listview">
  <li>Restaurants
    <ul>
      <li>French
        <ul>
          <li>Le Central</li>
          <li>Bistro Vandome</li>
          <li>Antoine's</li>
        </ul>
      </li>
      <li>Cajun and Creole
        <ul>
          <li>Bayou Bob's</li>
          <li>Pappadeaux</li>
          <li>Lucile's</li>
        </ul>
      </li>
      <li>American
        <ul>
          <li>Dixon's</li>
          <li>Vesta Dipping Grill</li>
          <li>Steuben's</li>
        </ul>
      </li>
    </ul>
  </li>
</ul>
```

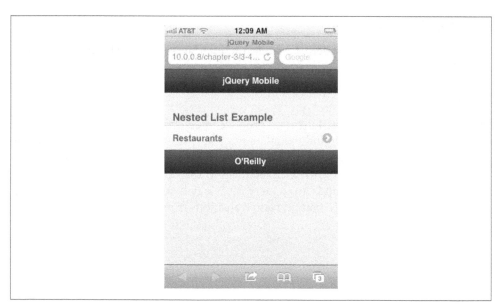

Figure 3-4. Nested list view (page 1)

Figure 3-5. Nested list view (page 2)

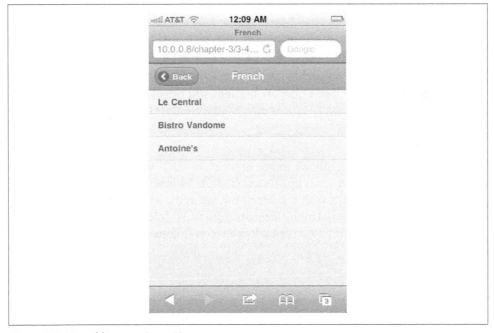

Figure 3-6. Nested list view (page 3)

List View Split Buttons

jQuery Mobile can produce a list of split buttons: buttons that are split into two different tappable areas. The main area is the widest, with a smaller area at the right of the button. Split buttons are commonly used in mobile user interfaces, and provide a convenient way of having two different functions in one list item: for example, to view a list item's details or to configure the item somehow, or as in the case of 3-5, to view a restaurant's details or to make reservations at the restaurant.

To create a split button, simply add two anchor tags to your list item.

Example 3-5. Creating split buttons

```
<li>French
  <ul>
    <li>
      <a href="lecentral.html">Le Central</a>
      <a href="reservations.php?restaurant=903">Make Reservations</a>
    </li>
    <li>
      <a href="bistrovandome.html">Bistro Vandome</a>
      <a href="reservations.php?restaurant=904">Make Reservations</a>
    </li>
    <li>
      <a href="antoines.html">Antoine's</a>
      <a href="reservations.php?restaurant=905">Make Reservations</a>
    </li>
  </ul>
</li>
```

jQuery Mobile will automatically assign the first anchor as the main button link, and the last anchor as the smaller area to the right, as shown in Figure 3-7.

You can have more than two anchor tags in a list item, but jQuery Mobile will only use the very first and the very last. Other anchor tags will be included in the main button as regular links.

Thumbnails and Icons

You can also specify a thumbnail image or icon for each list item by including the appropriate image in your markup (Example 3-6). Thumbnails are images that are meant to be displayed flush with the left of the list item, while icons are smaller and meant to be vertically centered in the list item. jQuery Mobile provides a CSS class that you can apply to an image to specify that it is an icon (Figure 3-8) and not a thumbnail (Figure 3-9).

Figure 3-7. List view with split buttons

Example 3-6. List view icons and thumbnails<ul data-role="listview">

```
<li>Restaurants
  <ul>
    <li>
      <a href="#">
        <img src="../images/icons/icon-french.png"
             alt="French flag icon"
             class="ui-li-icon">
        French
      </a>
      <ul>
        <li>
          <a href="lecentral.html">
            <img src="../images/logo-generic.png" alt="Le Central logo">
            Le Central
          </a>
          <a href="reservations.php?restaurant=403">Make Reservations</a>
        </li>
        <li>
          <a href="bistrovandome.html">
            <img src="../images/logo-generic.png" alt="Bistro Vandome logo">
            Bistro Vandome
          </a>
          <a href="reservations.php?restaurant=404">Make Reservations
          </a>
```

```
        </li>
        <li>
          <a href="antoines.html">
            <img src="../images/logo-generic.png" alt="Antoine's logo">
            Antoine's
          </a>
          <a href="reservations.php?restaurant=405">Make Reservations</a>
        </li>
      </ul>
    </li>
    <li>
      <a href="#">
        <img src="../images/icons/icon-cajun.png"
             alt="Cajun flag icon"
             class="ui-li-icon">
        Cajun
      </a>
      <ul>
        <li>Bayou Bob's</li>
        <li>Pappadeaux</li>
        <li>Lucile's</li>
      </ul>
    </li>
    <li>
      <a href="#">
        <img src="../images/icons/icon-american.png"
             alt="American flag icon"
             class="ui-li-icon">
        American
      </a>
      <ul>
        <li>Dixon's</li>
        <li>Vesta Dipping Grill</li>
        <li>Steuben's</li>
      </ul>
    </li>
  </ul>
  </li>
</ul>
```

 As of this writing, jQuery Mobile seems to expect icons and thumbnails to be contained within anchor tags within list items, even if the list item isn't meant to be tappable. Without the anchor tag, the formatting will not be correct. Since jQuery Mobile will ignore any link to "#", it's not a problem to include the anchor tag even when it is not semantically valid.

Figure 3-8. List view with icons

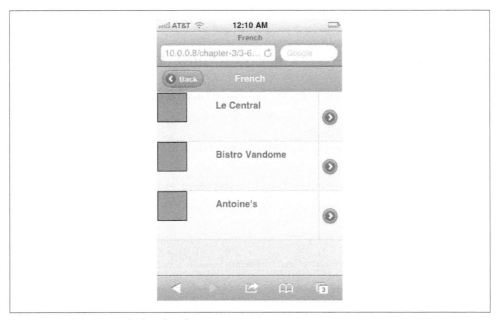

Figure 3-9. List view with thumbnails

Count Bubbles

Count bubbles are the icons in list views that show count information of the item in question. To include a count bubble with jQuery Mobile, add the markup and include the class `ui-li-count`, as shown in Example 3-7. The results are shown in Figures 3-10, 3-11, and 3-12.

Example 3-7. List item count bubbles

```
<ul data-role="listview">
  <li data-role="divider">Items<span class="ui-li-count">10</span></li>
  <li><a href="#">Restaurants</a><span class="ui-li-count">9</span>
    <ul>
      <li>
        <a href="#">
         <img src="../images/icons/icon-french.png"
              alt="French flag icon"
              class="ui-li-icon">
         French
         <span class="ui-li-count">3</span>
        </a>
        <ul>
          <li>
            <a href="lecentral.html">
              <img src="../images/logo-generic.png" alt="Le Central logo">
              Le Central
            </a>
            <span class="ui-li-count">9</span>
            <a href="reservations.php?restaurant=403">Make Reservations</a>
          </li>
          <li>
            <a href="bistrovandome.html">
              <img src="../images/logo-generic.png" alt="Bistro Vandome logo">
              Bistro Vandome
            </a>
            <a href="reservations.php?restaurant=404">Make Reservations</a>
          </li>
          <li>
            <a href="antoines.html">
              <img src="../images/logo-generic.png" alt="Antoine's logo">
              Antoine's
            </a>
            <a href="reservations.php?restaurant=405">Make Reservations</a>
          </li>
        </ul>
      </li>
      <li>
        <a href="#">
          <img src="../images/icons/icon-cajun.png"
              alt="Cajun icon"
              class="ui-li-icon">
          Cajun
          <span class="ui-li-count">3</span>
        </a>
        <ul>
```

```
        <li>Bayou Bob's</li>
        <li>Pappadeaux</li>
        <li>Lucile's</li>
      </ul>
    </li>
    <li>
      <a href="#">
        <img src="../images/icons/icon-american.png"
            alt="American flag icon"
            class="ui-li-icon">
        American
        <span class="ui-li-count">3</span>
      </a>
      <ul>
        <li>Dixon's</li>
        <li>Vesta Dipping Grill</li>
        <li>Steuben's</li>
      </ul>
    </li>
  </ul>
 </li>
</ul>
```

 As of this writing, count bubbles only work within anchor tags inside of list items, or within list view dividers (list items with `data-role="divider"` applied to them). In split buttons, count bubbles cannot be included in the last anchor tag.

Figure 3-10. List view count bubbles (page 1)

Figure 3-11. List view count bubbles (page 2)

Figure 3-12. List view count bubbles (page 3)

Under The Hood: Updating a List View

A list view is probably the most complex element that jQuery Mobile produces, and is also one of the most common that you'll use in your application.

jQuery Mobile list views are created using the `listview` widget. Like other jQuery widgets, the `listview` widget can expose methods for you to call after initialization. As of this writing, the `listview` widget exposes the `refresh` method, which you can use to update a list view. This is most useful when you have to add or remove items from a previously initialized list view (Example 3-8).

Example 3-8. Updating a list view with new items

```
<script>

// Initialize the list view
$("ul.twitter-feed").listview();

var updateTweets = function() {
  // Go get more tweets and prepend them to the list and then
  // refresh the list view.
  var strNewTweetsHtml = getNewTweets();
  $("ul.twitter-feed").prepend(strNewTweetsHtml).listview("refresh");
}

</script>
```

This demonstrates one of the benefits of the jQuery widget pattern: it attaches methods to DOM elements that you can call after initialization.

Toolbars

jQuery Mobile can produce several different toolbars. We've already seen the header and footer in our first example. jQuery Mobile can also produce navigation bars as well.

Navigation Bars

In a mobile user interface, navigation bars typically consist of a set of buttons that allow the user to navigate through the application views. Navigation bars can be included within the header, footer, or content areas of a jQuery Mobile page view. Depending on where it is included, jQuery Mobile will format the navigation bar appropriately.

To designate a navigation bar, apply the `data-role="navigation"` to a block level element like the HTML 5 nav element. Anchor tags contained within a designated navigation element will be formatted as a button group, and jQuery Mobile will handle changing the active and inactive states of the buttons automatically (Example 3-9). Figure 3-13 shows the result.

Example 3-9. Basic navigation bar

```
<section id="page1" data-role="page">
  <header data-role="header">
    <h1>jQuery Mobile</h1>
    <nav data-role="navbar">
        <a href="#" class="ui-btn-active">First</a>
        <a href="#">Second</a>
        <a href="#">Third</a>
        <a href="#">Fourth</a>
        <a href="#">Fifth</a>
    </nav>
  </header>
  <div class="content" data-role="content">
    <h3>Content</h3>
  </div>
  </div>
  <footer data-role="footer">
    <h3>O'Reilly</h3>
  </footer>
</section>
```

Figure 3-13. Basic navigation bar

The CSS class `ui-btn-active` specifies the active state of navigation buttons.

jQuery Mobile can also make the buttons of equal width. To do this, enclose the anchor tags within an unordered list (Example 3-10). Figure 3-14 shows the result.

Example 3-10. Formatted navigation bar

```
<nav data-role="navbar">
    <ul>
        <li><a href="#" class="ui-btn-active">First</a></li>
        <li><a href="#">Second</a></li>
        <li><a href="#">Third</a></li>
        <li><a href="#">Fourth</a></li>
        <li><a href="#">Fifth</a></li>
    </ul>
</nav>
```

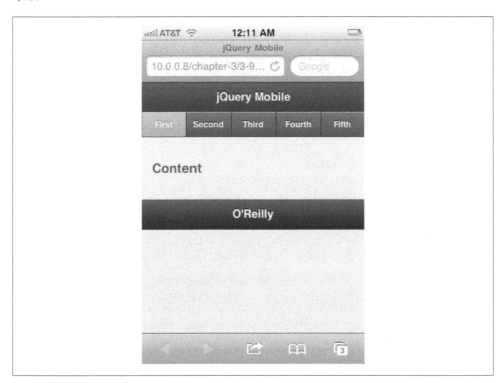

Figure 3-14. Formatted navigation bar

jQuery Mobile will fit up to five items in a formatted navigation bar. If more elements are included, jQuery Mobile will stack them into two columns. For example, see Example 3-11 and Figure 3-15.

Example 3-11. Navigation bar with stacked buttons

```
<nav data-role="navbar">
    <ul>
        <li><a href="#" class="ui-btn-active">First</a></li>
        <li><a href="#">Second</a></li>
        <li><a href="#">Third</a></li>
        <li><a href="#">Fourth</a></li>
        <li><a href="#">Fifth</a></li>
        <li><a href="#">Sixth</a></li>
    </ul>
</nav>
```

Figure 3-15. Navigation bar with stacked buttons

Positioning the Header and Footer

jQuery Mobile can dynamically position the header and footer toolbars in three ways:

Standard

> The toolbars are presented according to the document flow, scrolling into and out of the viewport as the user scrolls through data. This is the default.

Fixed

> The header and footer will appear at the top and bottom of the viewport and remain there as the user scrolls. Tapping on the screen will cause them to return to their regular position in the document flow.

Fullscreen

> The header and footer will appear within the viewport and stay present as the user scrolls, regardless of where the user is in the content. Tapping on the screen will hide them. Essentially, the header and footer are removed from the document flow and are always dynamically positioned at the top and bottom of the viewport.

To create a fixed header and footer, apply the `data-position="fixed"` attribute to them (Example 3-12).

Example 3-12. Fixed header and footer

```
<section id="page1" data-role="page">
  <header data-role="header" data-position="fixed">
     <h1>jQuery Mobile</h1>
  </header>
  <div class="content" data-role="content">
    <h3>Content area.</h3>
  </div>
  </div>
  <footer data-role="footer" data-position="fixed">
    <h3>O'Reilly</h3>
  </footer>
</section>
```

To create the fullscreen header and footer, apply the `data-fullscreen="true"` attribute to the element designated with the `data-role="page"`, and also apply the `data- position ="fixed"` attribute to the header and footer elements:

```
    <section id="page1" data-role="page" data-fullscreen="true">
      <header data-role="header" data-position="fixed">
         <h1>jQuery Mobile</h1>
      </header>
      <div class="content" data-role="content">
        <h3>Content area.</h3>
      </div>
      </div>
      <footer data-role="footer" data-position="fixed">
        <h3>O'Reilly</h3>
      </footer>
    </section>
```

Dynamically positioned toolbars will obscure content while they are visible (for example, see Figure 3-16).

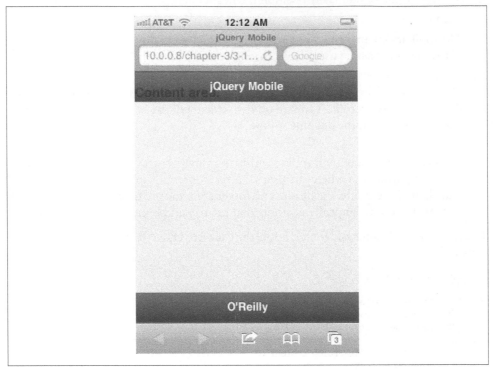

Figure 3-16. Dynamically positioned header and footer

Buttons

jQuery Mobile will automatically create stylized buttons out of regular form buttons, whether they be created with the input tag or the button tag. jQuery Mobile can also create buttons out of simple anchor links, by applying the `data-role="button"` to them.

By default, buttons will stretch to fit the width of their containing element. By applying the `data-inline="true"` attribute to a button, you can create inline buttons that are only as big as their content requires (Example 3-13, Figure 3-17).

Example 3-13. Button, button, who's got the button?

```
<section id="page1" data-role="page">
  <header data-role="header"><h1>jQuery Mobile</h1></header>
  <div class="content" data-role="content">
    <h3>Buttons</h3>
    <a href="#" data-role="button">Link-based button</a>
    <input type="submit" value="submit" data-inline="true">
    <input type="reset" value="reset" data-inline="true">
  </div>
  </div>
  <footer data-role="footer"><h1>O'Reilly</h1></footer>
</section>
```

Figure 3-17. Button, button, who's got the button?

 As of this writing, the jQuery Mobile documentation states that by applying the data-inline="true" attribute to a containing element, all buttons contained therein will be rendered inline. This is not working. The data-inline="true" attribute must be applied to each individual button. See *http://jquerymobile.com/demos/1.0a4.1/docs/buttons/buttons-inline.html* for more information. I expect this bug will be fixed by release 1.0.

Button Control Groups

Buttons can also be grouped together in control groups, creating a group of buttons on one bar. Just wrap the buttons in a containing element and apply the data-role= "controlgroup" to that container.

By default, these control groups form a vertical list, but if you apply the data-type= "horizontal" attribute to the container (as I have done in Example 3-14), the buttons will be rendered inline (as illustrated in Figure 3-18).

Example 3-14. Button control groups

```
<section id="page1" data-role="page">
  <header data-role="header"><h1>jQuery Mobile</h1></header>
  <div class="content" data-role="content">
    <h3>Control Group Buttons</h3>
    <div data-role="controlgroup">
      <a href="#" data-role="button">Yes</a>
      <a href="#" data-role="button">No</a>
      <a href="#" data-role="button">Cancel</a>
    </div>
    <div data-role="controlgroup" data-type="horizontal">
      <a href="#" data-role="button">Yes</a>
      <a href="#" data-role="button">No</a>
      <a href="#" data-role="button">Cancel</a>
    </div>
  </div>
  </div>
  <footer data-role="footer"><h1>O'Reilly</h1></footer>
</section>
```

Figure 3-18. Button control groups

Control group buttons do not have the same functionality as radio buttons. More than one button in a control group can be active at a time.

Button Icons

Often you will need icons in your buttons, and jQuery Mobile comes with a variety of icons. You can also control the position of the icon.

To specify the icon of a button, apply the `data-icon` attribute. The `data-icon` attribute has the following valid values (Table 3-1).

Table 3-1. Valid data-icon values

Value	Icon
alert	
arrow-d	
arrow-l	
arrow-r	
arrow-u	
back	
check	
delete	
forward	
gear	
grid	
home	
info	
minus	
plus	
refresh	
search	
star	

You can specify the position of the icon using the `data-iconpos` attribute. Valid values are shown in Table 3-2.

Table 3-2. Valid data-iconpos values

Value	Result
bottom	Below the text, centered
left	Left side of button
notext	Hides the text, displaying only the icon
right	Right side of button
top	Above text, centered

Example 3-15 shows the code for adding some of these button icons, and the result is shown in Figure 3-19.

Example 3-15. Button icons

```
<section id="page1" data-role="page">
  <header data-role="header"><h1>jQuery Mobile</h1></header>
  <div class="content" data-role="content">
    <h3>Button Icons</h3>
    <div data-role="controlgroup" data-type="horizontal" data-inline="true">
      <a href="#" data-role="button" data-icon="home" data-iconpos="left">Home</a>
      <a href="#" data-role="button" data-icon="gear"
         data-iconpos="left">Configure</a>
      <a href="#" data-role="button" data-icon="search"
         data-iconpos="left">Search</a>
    </div>
  </div>
  </div>
  <footer data-role="footer"><h1>O'Reilly</h1></footer>
</section>
```

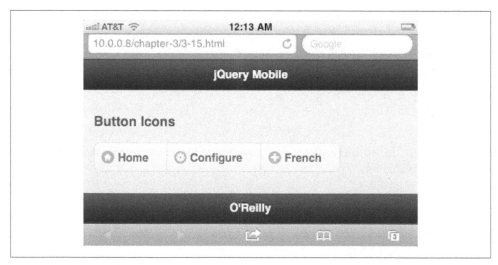

Figure 3-19. Button icons

Custom Icons

Though jQuery Mobile comes with its own icons, you can easily implement your own icons using CSS and a custom data-icon attribute. If you specify a value for data-icon that is not one of the valid values, jQuery Mobile will still create the button but will apply to it a custom CSS class that will consist of the value for data-icon prepended by *ui-icon-*. For example, if you specified `data-icon="flagicons-french"` then jQuery Mobile would generate the button and create within it a span tag with the CSS class `ui-icon-flagicons-french`.

jQuery Mobile's button icon classes are all designed around icons that are 18 × 18 pixels square. If you will be using jQuery Mobile's theming system (see Chapter 4), you should probably save your icons in PNG format with alpha transparency.

Form Elements

jQuery Mobile will automatically enhance native form elements with touch-enhanced user interface components.

Begin by marking up your form semantically. Be sure to include labels for your elements as appropriate, and wrap all form fields within a valid form tag.

If you wish to visually group form elements together within a form, apply the `data-role="fieldcontain"` attribute to an element wrapping the elements in question. Fieldsets or divs are ideal for this.

jQuery Mobile will automatically handle the form submission via AJAX, and will attempt to integrate the server response into the DOM of the application, providing transitions as expected. If you wish to disallow jQuery Mobile's AJAX form handling for a given form, apply the attribute `data-ajax="false"` to the form tag.

Finally, if you don't want jQuery Mobile to enhance a form element or an entire form, apply the `data-role="none"` attribute to the element or form tag in question.

Accessing Form Elements with JavaScript

As with other page elements, jQuery Mobile form elements are governed by various jQuery Widgets. One of the main benefits of the jQuery Widget pattern in this case is that it allows you to have access to widget methods even after the form element has been initialized. You can use exposed widget methods to do various useful things: read and set selected values, change information, enable and disable elements, manually initialize elements or return them to their unenhanced state, and so forth.

Checkboxes and Radio Buttons

jQuery Mobile will automatically enhance checkboxes and radio buttons into button-like elements in the user interface. Like other buttons, you can group them together into control groups using `data-role="controlgroup"` on a containing element. By default, control groups are vertical stacks of buttons that stretch to the full width of their containing element. To create a horizontal control group, use the `data-type="horizontal"` attribute, as I have done in Example 3-16. Figure 3-20 shows the result.

Example 3-16. Checkboxes and radio buttons

```
<section id="page1" data-role="page">
  <header data-role="header"><h1>jQuery Mobile</h1></header>
  <div class="content" data-role="content">
    <h3>Checkboxes and Radio Buttons</h3>
    <form id="myform" action="formprocessor.php" method="post">
      <div data-role="fieldcontain">
        <fieldset data-role="controlgroup">
          <legend>Filter Restaurants By:</legend>
          <input type="checkbox" name="checkbox-french" id="checkbox-french">
          <label for="checkbox-french">French</label>
          <input type="checkbox" name="checkbox-italian" id="checkbox-italian">
          <label for="checkbox-italian">Italian</label>
          <input type="checkbox" name="checkbox-greek" id="checkbox-greek">
          <label for="checkbox-greek">Greek</label>
        </fieldset>
      <div data-role="fieldcontain">
        <fieldset data-role="controlgroup" data-type="horizontal">
          <legend>Select a Language:</legend>
          <input type="radio" name="radio-language" id="radio-french">
          <label for="radio-french">French</label>
          <input type="radio" name="radio-language" id="radio-italian"
                 checked="checked">
          <label for="radio-italian">Italian</label>
          <input type="radio" name="radio-language" id="radio-greek">
          <label for="radio-greek">Greek</label>
        </fieldset>
      </div>
    </div>
  </form>
  </div>
  <footer data-role="footer"><h1>O'Reilly</h1></footer>
</section>
```

Figure 3-20. Checkboxes and radio buttons

Methods

jQuery Mobile uses the `checkboxradio` widget to manage checkboxes and radio buttons. You can use `checkboxradio` to enable, disable, or refresh a given checkbox or radio button (Example 3-17).

Example 3-17. The checkboxradio method

```
<script>
// Disable a button
$("#checkbox-french").checkboxradio("disable");

// Enable a disabled button
$("#checkbox-italian").checkboxradio("enable");

// Manually activate a button and refresh its UI state
$("#radio-greek").attr("checked", true).checkboxradio("refresh");
</script>
```

Flip Toggle

Flip toggles or switches are common mobile user interface elements. They allow the user to toggle between two values ("on" and "off", for example). The user can flip the toggle by either sliding the toggle back and forth or by tapping on the toggle.

jQuery Mobile uses the `select` HTML form element to create flip toggles. Simply create a `select` element with two options, and apply the `data-role="slider"` attribute to it, as shown in Example 3-18. Figure 3-21 shows the result.

Example 3-18. Flip toggle

```
<section id="page1" data-role="page">
  <header data-role="header"><h1>jQuery Mobile</h1></header>
  <div class="content" data-role="content">
    <h3>Checkboxes and Radio Buttons</h3>
    <form id="myform" action="formprocessor.php" method="post">
      <div data-role="fieldcontain">
        <label for="slider-music">Ambient Music</label>
        <select name="slider-music" id="slider-music" data-role="slider">
          <option value="on">On</option>
          <option value="off">Off</option>
        </select>
      </div>
    </form>
  </div>
  <footer data-role="footer"><h1>O'Reilly</h1></footer>
</section>
```

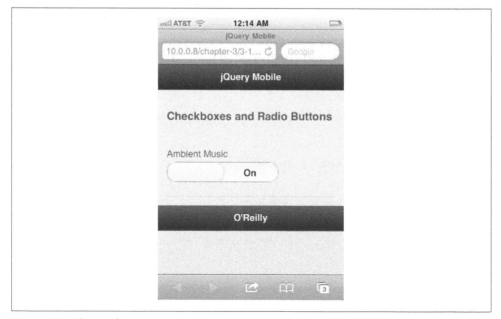

Figure 3-21. Flip toggle

Methods

jQuery Mobile uses the `slider` widget to handle toggles. Example 3-19 shows how to access a toggle directly.

Example 3-19. The slider method

```
<script>
$(document).ready(function() {

  var mySlider = $("#slider-music");

  // Disable a slider
  mySlider.slider('disable');

  // Enable a slider
  mySlider.slider("enable");

  // Manually flip a slider and update its UI state
  // (just flipping it will not automatically update the UI)
  mySlider[0].selectedIndex = 1;
  mySlider.slider("refresh");

})
</script>
```

Input Fields and Textareas

jQuery Mobile handles input fields and textareas as well. It will visually enhance the elements with rounded corners and shadows by default, though this can easily be changed (see Chapter 4).

Input fields can apply a `type` attribute and use several of the new values defined in HTML 5 to help the user by displaying the correct kind of keyboard to use. For example, an input with a `type="number"` will show the numeric keyboard in most mobile devices, and so forth.

Textareas will grow in height as the user types in input. This is to avoid the creation of scrollbars.

Methods

jQuery Mobile uses the `textinput` plug-in to handle textareas and input fields (Example 3-20).

Example 3-20. The textinput method

```
<script>
$(document).ready(function() {

  // Disable an input
  $("#myinput").textinput('disable');

  // Enable an input
  $("#myotherinput").textinput("enable");

})
</script>
```

Search Fields

Search fields are styled inputs. They start out with a search icon (a magnifying glass) in the left of the input field. As the user begins to type, a clear icon (an "x") appears in the right of the input field. Tapping on the stop icon will clear the user's input from the field.

To create a search field, simply apply a `type="search"` attribute to an input field, as shown in Example 3-21. Figure 3-22 shows the result.

Example 3-21. Search input

```
<section id="page1" data-role="page">
  <header data-role="header"><h1>jQuery Mobile</h1></header>
  <div class="content" data-role="content">
    <h3>Search Input</h3>
    <form id="myform" action="formprocessor.php" method="post">
      <div data-role="fieldcontain">
        <label for="search-restaurants">Search Restaurants:</label>
        <input type="search" name="search-restaurants" id="search-restaurants" />
      </div>
    </form>
  </div>
  <footer data-role="footer"><h1>O'Reilly</h1></footer>
</section>
```

Methods

The search input is just a styled input field, so it uses the `textinput` widget (see Example 3-20).

Figure 3-22. Search input

Select Menus

Select menus are one of the more heavily progressively enhanced elements in the jQuery Mobile library. jQuery Mobile can either attempt to use the platform's native select widget, or it can produce a custom styled select menu.

The custom styled select menu has many benefits over using the native select widget. On some platforms, the native select widget is missing important features (for example, Android is missing support for optgroup), and the custom styled select menu restores these features. The custom styled select menu also adds extra features, like multiple select support, and it is easier to style so it matches the visual theme of your application.

By default, jQuery Mobile will attempt to use the native select widget. You don't need to do anything, just create your select element with its options. To force jQuery Mobile to create a custom styled select menu, apply the data-native-menu="false" attribute to the select element, as shown in Example 3-22. Figure 3-23 shows the result.

Example 3-22. Native select menu

```
<section id="page1" data-role="page">
  <header data-role="header"><h1>jQuery Mobile</h1></header>
  <div class="content" data-role="content">
    <h3>Native Select Menu Demonstration</h3>
    <form id="myform" action="formprocessor.php" method="post">
      <div data-role="fieldcontain">
        <label for="select-restaurants">Select Your Restaurants:</label>
        <select id="select-restaurants" name="select-restaurants">
            <option value="lecentral">Le Central</option>
            <option value="bistrovandome">Bistro Vandome</option>
            <option value="antoines">Antoine's</option>
        </select>
      </div>
    </form>
  </div>
  <footer data-role="footer"><h1>O'Reilly</h1></footer>
</section>
```

Figure 3-23. Native select menu

Custom Styled Select Menus

Custom Styled Select Menus have several important features:

Disabled Elements. You can specify disabled elements by using the `disabled` attribute on any `option` tag.

Multiple Selections. The custom styled select menu supports multiple selections. To add this feature, add the `multiple` attribute to the `select` element. jQuery Mobile will then add the following features to the menu:

- The pop-up menu will contain a header that will contain a close button and the placeholder text (see Placeholders, below). Clicking on the close button will close the menu. This allows us to keep the pop-up menu open so the user can make multiple selects; ordinarily, once you select one thing from a select menu it closes automatically.

- Checkboxes will appear to the right of each item, indicating whether or not the item has been selected.

- A counter bubble will appear in the select button when two or more items are selected.

- When the user closes the pop-up menu, the text of each selected item will be added to the select button. If the text is too long to fit in the button, it will be truncated.

- If the select list is long, jQuery Mobile will display it as a separate window rather than a pop up, making it easier for the user to scroll.

 As of this writing, the multiple selection feature has a few minor bugs. Be sure to test it thoroughly in your application to verify it is functioning as expected.

Optgroups. jQuery Mobile will interpret `optgroup` tags that you use to group your `option` tags together and create headers dividing the resulting list in the pop up.

Placeholders. You can specify a placeholder in one of three ways: leave an `option` tag empty of both text and value, leave an `option` tag empty of a value (but still have text), or apply a `data-placeholder="true"` attribute to an `option` tag.

If there is text in the placeholder option, jQuery Mobile will display it in the select button.

In Example 3-23 we put all of this together, and show the results in Figure 3-24.

Example 3-23. Custom select menu

```
<section id="page1" data-role="page">
  <header data-role="header"><h1>jQuery Mobile</h1></header>
  <div class="content" data-role="content">
    <h3>Select Menu Demonstration</h3>
    <form id="myform" action="formprocessor.php" method="post">
      <div data-role="fieldcontain">
```

```
    <label for="select-restaurants">Select Your Restaurants:</label>
    <select id="select-restaurants"
            name="select-restaurants"
            data-native-menu="false"
            multiple="multiple">
      <option value="choose" data-placeholder="true">Choose...</option>
      <optgroup label="French">
        <option value="lecentral">Le Central</option>
        <option value="bistrovandome">Bistro Vandome</option>
        <option value="antoines">Antoine's</option>
      </optgroup>
      <optgroup label="Cajun">
        <option value="bayoubobs">Bayou Bob's</option>
        <option value="pappadeaux" disabled="disabled">Pappadeaux</option>
        <option value="luciles">Lucile's</option>
      </optgroup>
    </select>
  </div>

  </form>
 </div>
 <footer data-role="footer"><h1>O'Reilly</h1></footer>
</section>
```

Figure 3-24. Custom select menu

Methods

jQuery Mobile uses the `selectmenu` widget to handle select menus (Example 3-24).

Example 3-24. The selectmenu method

```
<script>
$(document).ready(function() {
    mySelect = $("#select-restaurants");

    // Disable a select menu
    mySelect.selectmenu("disable");

    // Enable a select menu
    mySelect.selectmenu("enable");

    // Manually open a select menu
    mySelect.selectmenu("open");

    // Manually close a select menu
    mySelect.selectmenu("close");

    // Manually select an item and refresh the UI state
    mySelect[0].selectedIndex = 2;
    mySelect.selectmenu("refresh");

    // Force a rebuild of the select menu
    // Useful if you have dynamically added or removed options
    mySelect.selectmenu("refresh", true);
});
</script>
```

Sliders

Sliders are elements that enable users to select from a range of values by sliding a cursor back and forth.

To create a slider, simply apply a `type="range"` attribute to your input field, as shown in Example 3-25. You can then provide min and max attributes. Figure 3-25 shows the result. (As of this writing, the slider does not support a "step" attribute.)

Example 3-25. Slider element

```
<section id="page1" data-role="page">
  <header data-role="header"><h1>jQuery Mobile</h1></header>
  <div class="content" data-role="content">
    <h3>Slider Demonstration</h3>
    <form id="myform" action="formprocessor.php" method="post">
      <div data-role="fieldcontain">
          <input type="range" id="slider" name="slider" min="0" max="500">
      </div>
    </form>
  </div>
```

```
    <footer data-role="footer"><h1>O'Reilly</h1></footer>
</section>
```

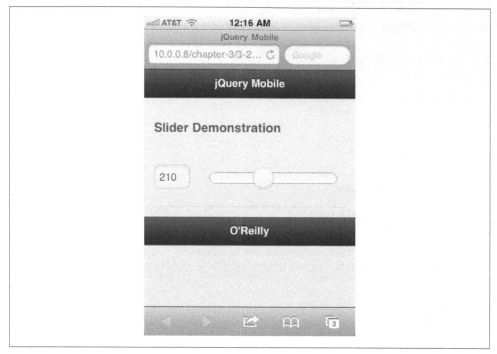

Figure 3-25. Slider element

The user can either slide the slider back and forth, or enter a value in the input field and the slider will automatically update.

Methods

The slider uses the slider method (Example 3-26).

Example 3-26. The slider method

```
<script>
$(document).ready(function() {

    // Disable a slider
    $("#slider").slider("disable");

    // Enable a slider
    $("#slider").slider("enable");

    // Manually set a slider's value and refresh the state of the UI
    $("#slider").val(100).slider("refresh");
})
</script>
```

Layout Grids

jQuery Mobile has a set of layout grids built in, ranging from two to five columns. Layout grids are useful when you have smaller elements like buttons or form fields that you need to lay out with more precision.

Layout grids are based on a div structure: create a div to contain the grid, and then add the cell divs inside. The containing div is given a class ui-grid class: ui-grid-a for 2 columns, ui-grid-b for three columns, and so forth, all the way to ui-grid d for 5 columns. Cell divs are given ui-block classes based on their order: ui-block-a for first, ui-block-b for second, and so forth, all the way up to ui-block-e for fifth.

Multiple rows are handled by adding more cell divs, which should be classed so that each column should have its own ui-block class (Example 3-27). Figure 3-26 and Figure 3-27 show the result.

Example 3-27. Layout grids

```
<!DOCTYPE html>
<html>
  <head>
    <title>jQuery Mobile Application</title>
    <link rel="stylesheet" href="http://code.jquery.com/mobile/1.0a4.1/jquery.mobile-1.0a4.1.min.css" />
    <script src="http://code.jquery.com/jquery-1.5.2.min.js"></script>
    <script src="http://code.jquery.com/mobile/1.0a4.1/jquery.mobile-1.0a4.1.min.js"></script>
    <style>
.content div div p {
    background-color: #ccc;
    height: 50px;
    border: 1px solid #333;
    margin: 0px;
}
    </style>
  </head>
  <body>
    <section id="page1" data-role="page">
      <header data-role="header"><h1>jQuery Mobile</h1></header>
      <div class="content" data-role="content">
        <h4>2 Colums</h4>
        <div class="ui-grid-b">
          <div class="ui-block-a"><p>Block A</p></div>
          <div class="ui-block-b"><p>Block B</p></div>
        </div>

        <h4>3 Columns</h4>
        <div class="ui-grid-b">
          <div class="ui-block-a"><p>Block A</p></div>
          <div class="ui-block-b"><p>Block B</p></div>
          <div class="ui-block-c"><p>Block C</p></div>
        </div>

        <h4>4 Columns</h4>
        <div class="ui-grid-c">
```

```
    <div class="ui-block-a"><p>Block A</p></div>
    <div class="ui-block-b"><p>Block B</p></div>
    <div class="ui-block-c"><p>Block C</p></div>
    <div class="ui-block-d"><p>Block D</p></div>
</div>

<h4>5 Columns</h4>
<div class="ui-grid-d">
    <div class="ui-block-a"><p>Block A</p></div>
    <div class="ui-block-b"><p>Block B</p></div>
    <div class="ui-block-c"><p>Block C</p></div>
    <div class="ui-block-d"><p>Block D</p></div>
    <div class="ui-block-e"><p>Block E</p></div>
</div>


<h4>2 Rows of 3 Columns</h4>
<div class="ui-grid-d">
    <div class="ui-block-a"><p>Block A</p></div>
    <div class="ui-block-b"><p>Block B</p></div>
    <div class="ui-block-c"><p>Block C</p></div>
    <div class="ui-block-a"><p>Block A</p></div>
    <div class="ui-block-b"><p>Block B</p></div>
    <div class="ui-block-c"><p>Block C</p></div>
</div>

</div>
<footer data-role="footer"><h1>O'Reilly</h1></footer>
</section>

</body>
</html>
```

In Figure 3-26 and Figure 3-27, I have included the entire document rather than just the page view, to show the CSS rule I added to make the blocks visible.

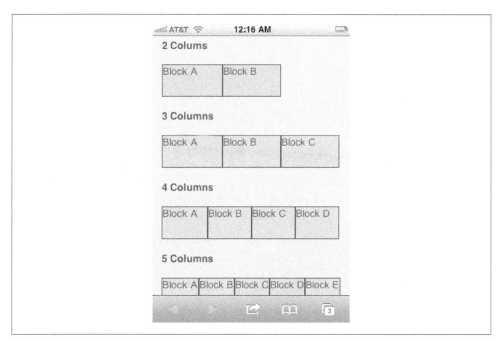

Figure 3-26. Layout grids 1

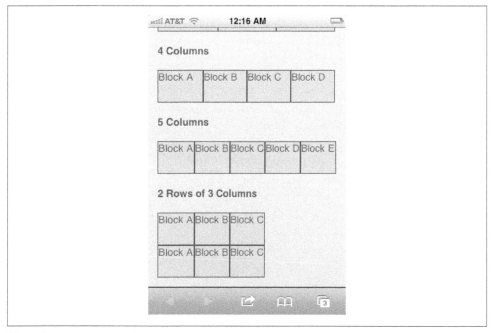

Figure 3-27. Layout grids 2

CHAPTER 4

Theming jQuery Mobile

jQuery Mobile includes a sophisticated theming system. Built with mobile applications in mind, it makes extensive use of CSS 3 capabilities to produce rounded corners, drop shadows, and gradients, making it lightweight and easily extensible.

The theming framework separates the ideas of color and texture from standard layout concepts of padding and dimension, so it's possible to change the former without necessarily having to change the latter. This gives the framework great mix-and-match flexibility for producing wide variety of visual designs.

Themes and Swatches

In jQuery Mobile, a "theme" is a unified visual design applied across the interface. In practical terms, a theme specifies everything from fonts to drop shadows to colors.

In keeping with the idea of separating layout from color and texture, a jQuery Mobile theme can have multiple "swatches." A swatch is a unified color concept governing the colors of background, text, shadows, iconography, etc.

The default jQuery Mobile theme includes five swatches (called a, b, c, d, and e). Each swatch provides different visual emphasis, with swatch a being the most visually emphatic (typically white text on a black background), and swatch d being much softer. Swatch e is an "error" swatch.

jQuery Mobile defaults to swatch c in most cases, but it is easy to specify a different swatch using the `data-theme` attribute. The `data-theme` attribute can be applied to any enhanced element and will cascade down through child elements (Example 4-1). Figures 4-1, 4-2, 4-3, 4-4, 4-5, and 4-6 show the results.

Example 4-1. Swatch browsing application

```html
<section id="swatch-default" data-role="page">
  <header data-role="header"><h1>jQuery Mobile</h1></header>
  <div class="content" data-role="content">
    <h3>Default Swatch</h3>
    <ul data-role="listview">
        <li><a href="#swatch-a">View swatch a</a></li>
        <li><a href="#swatch-b">View swatch b</a></li>
        <li><a href="#swatch-c">View swatch c</a></li>
        <li><a href="#swatch-d">View swatch d</a></li>
        <li><a href="#swatch-e">View swatch e</a></li>
    </ul>
    <p>Some sample form elements and buttons:</p>
    <form  action="formprocessor.php" method="post">
      <div data-role="fieldcontain">
        <label for="select-restaurants">Select Your Restaurants:</label>
        <select id="select-restaurants"
                name="select-restaurants"
                data-native-menu="false"
                multiple="multiple">
          <option value="choose" data-placeholder="true">Choose...</option>
          <optgroup label="French">
            <option value="lecentral">Le Central</option>
            <option value="bistrovandome">Bistro Vandome</option>
            <option value="antoines">Antoine's</option>
          </optgroup>
          <optgroup label="Cajun">
            <option value="bayoubobs">Bayou Bob's</option>
            <option value="pappadeaux" disabled="disabled">Pappadeaux</option>
            <option value="luciles">Lucile's</option>
          </optgroup>
        </select>
      </div>
    </form>
    <div data-role="controlgroup" data-type="horizontal">
      <a href="#" data-role="button">Yes</a>
      <a href="#" data-role="button">No</a>
      <a href="#" data-role="button">Cancel</a>
    </div>
  </div>
  </div>
  <footer data-role="footer"><h1>O'Reilly</h1></footer>
</section>

<section id="swatch-a" data-role="page" data-theme="a">
  <header data-role="header"><h1>jQuery Mobile</h1></header>
  <div class="content" data-role="content">
    <h3>Swatch A</h3>
    <ul data-role="listview">
        <li><a href="#swatch-default">View default swatch</a></li>
        <li><a href="#swatch-b">View swatch b</a></li>
        <li><a href="#swatch-c">View swatch c</a></li>
        <li><a href="#swatch-d">View swatch d</a></li>
        <li><a href="#swatch-e">View swatch e</a></li>
    </ul>
```

```
    <p>Some sample form elements and buttons:</p>
    <form  action="formprocessor.php" method="post">
      <div data-role="fieldcontain">
        <label for="select-restaurants">Select Your Restaurants:</label>
        <select id="select-restaurants"
                name="select-restaurants"
                data-native-menu="false"
                multiple="multiple">
          <option value="choose" data-placeholder="true">Choose...</option>
          <optgroup label="French">
            <option value="lecentral">Le Central</option>
            <option value="bistrovandome">Bistro Vandome</option>
            <option value="antoines">Antoine's</option>
          </optgroup>
          <optgroup label="Cajun">
            <option value="bayoubobs">Bayou Bob's</option>
            <option value="pappadeaux" disabled="disabled">Pappadeaux</option>
            <option value="luciles">Lucile's</option>
          </optgroup>
        </select>
      </div>
    </form>
    <div data-role="controlgroup" data-type="horizontal">
      <a href="#" data-role="button">Yes</a>
      <a href="#" data-role="button">No</a>
      <a href="#" data-role="button">Cancel</a>
    </div>
  </div>
  </div>
  <footer data-role="footer"><h1>O'Reilly</h1></footer>
</section>

<section id="swatch-b" data-role="page" data-theme="b">
  <header data-role="header"><h1>jQuery Mobile</h1></header>
  <div class="content" data-role="content">
    <h3>Swatch B</h3>
    <ul data-role="listview">
        <li><a href="#swatch-default">View default swatch</a></li>
        <li><a href="#swatch-a">View swatch a</a></li>
        <li><a href="#swatch-c">View swatch c</a></li>
        <li><a href="#swatch-d">View swatch d</a></li>
        <li><a href="#swatch-e">View swatch e</a></li>
    </ul>
    <p>Some sample form elements and buttons:</p>
    <form  action="formprocessor.php" method="post">
      <div data-role="fieldcontain">
        <label for="select-restaurants">Select Your Restaurants:</label>
        <select id="select-restaurants"
                name="select-restaurants"
                data-native-menu="false"
                multiple="multiple">
          <option value="choose" data-placeholder="true">Choose...</option>
          <optgroup label="French">
            <option value="lecentral">Le Central</option>
            <option value="bistrovandome">Bistro Vandome</option>
```

```
                <option value="antoines">Antoine's</option>
              </optgroup>
              <optgroup label="Cajun">
                <option value="bayoubobs">Bayou Bob's</option>
                <option value="pappadeaux" disabled="disabled">Pappadeaux</option>
                <option value="luciles">Lucile's</option>
              </optgroup>
            </select>
          </div>
        </form>
        <div data-role="controlgroup" data-type="horizontal">
          <a href="#" data-role="button">Yes</a>
          <a href="#" data-role="button">No</a>
          <a href="#" data-role="button">Cancel</a>
        </div>
      </div>
      </div>
      <footer data-role="footer"><h1>O'Reilly</h1></footer>
    </section>

    <section id="swatch-c" data-role="page" data-theme="c">
      <header data-role="header"><h1>jQuery Mobile</h1></header>
      <div class="content" data-role="content">
        <h3>Swatch C</h3>
        <ul data-role="listview">
            <li><a href="#swatch-default">View default swatch</a></li>
            <li><a href="#swatch-a">View swatch a</a></li>
            <li><a href="#swatch-b">View swatch b</a></li>
            <li><a href="#swatch-d">View swatch d</a></li>
            <li><a href="#swatch-e">View swatch e</a></li>
        </ul>
        <p>Some sample form elements and buttons:</p>
        <form  action="formprocessor.php" method="post">
          <div data-role="fieldcontain">
            <label for="select-restaurants">Select Your Restaurants:</label>
            <select id="select-restaurants"
                    name="select-restaurants"
                    data-native-menu="false"
                    multiple="multiple">
              <option value="choose" data-placeholder="true">Choose...</option>
              <optgroup label="French">
                <option value="lecentral">Le Central</option>
                <option value="bistrovandome">Bistro Vandome</option>
                <option value="antoines">Antoine's</option>
              </optgroup>
              <optgroup label="Cajun">
                <option value="bayoubobs">Bayou Bob's</option>
                <option value="pappadeaux" disabled="disabled">Pappadeaux</option>
                <option value="luciles">Lucile's</option>
              </optgroup>
            </select>
          </div>
        </form>
        <div data-role="controlgroup" data-type="horizontal">
          <a href="#" data-role="button">Yes</a>
```

```html
        <a href="#" data-role="button">No</a>
        <a href="#" data-role="button">Cancel</a>
      </div>
   </div>
   </div>
   <footer data-role="footer"><h1>O'Reilly</h1></footer>
</section>

<section id="swatch-d" data-role="page" data-theme="d">
   <header data-role="header"><h1>jQuery Mobile</h1></header>
   <div class="content" data-role="content">
     <h3>Swatch D</h3>
     <ul data-role="listview">
         <li><a href="#swatch-default">View default swatch</a></li>
         <li><a href="#swatch-a">View swatch a</a></li>
         <li><a href="#swatch-b">View swatch b</a></li>
         <li><a href="#swatch-c">View swatch c</a></li>
         <li><a href="#swatch-e">View swatch e</a></li>
     </ul>
     <p>Some sample form elements and buttons:</p>
     <form  action="formprocessor.php" method="post">
       <div data-role="fieldcontain">
         <label for="select-restaurants">Select Your Restaurants:</label>
         <select id="select-restaurants"
                 name="select-restaurants"
                 data-native-menu="false"
                 multiple="multiple">
           <option value="choose" data-placeholder="true">Choose...</option>
           <optgroup label="French">
             <option value="lecentral">Le Central</option>
             <option value="bistrovandome">Bistro Vandome</option>
             <option value="antoines">Antoine's</option>
           </optgroup>
           <optgroup label="Cajun">
             <option value="bayoubobs">Bayou Bob's</option>
             <option value="pappadeaux" disabled="disabled">Pappadeaux</option>
             <option value="luciles">Lucile's</option>
           </optgroup>
         </select>
       </div>
     </form>
     <div data-role="controlgroup" data-type="horizontal">
       <a href="#" data-role="button">Yes</a>
       <a href="#" data-role="button">No</a>
       <a href="#" data-role="button">Cancel</a>
     </div>
   </div>
   </div>
   <footer data-role="footer"><h1>O'Reilly</h1></footer>
</section>

<section id="swatch-e" data-role="page" data-theme="e">
   <header data-role="header"><h1>jQuery Mobile</h1></header>
   <div class="content" data-role="content">
     <h3>Swatch E</h3>
```

```
<ul data-role="listview">
    <li><a href="#swatch-default">View default swatch</a></li>
    <li><a href="#swatch-a">View swatch a</a></li>
    <li><a href="#swatch-b">View swatch b</a></li>
    <li><a href="#swatch-c">View swatch c</a></li>
    <li><a href="#swatch-d">View swatch d</a></li>
</ul>
<p>Some sample form elements and buttons:</p>
<form  action="formprocessor.php" method="post">
  <div data-role="fieldcontain">
    <label for="select-restaurants">Select Your Restaurants:</label>
    <select id="select-restaurants"
            name="select-restaurants"
            data-native-menu="false"
            multiple="multiple">
      <option value="choose" data-placeholder="true">Choose...</option>
      <optgroup label="French">
        <option value="lecentral">Le Central</option>
        <option value="bistrovandome">Bistro Vandome</option>
        <option value="antoines">Antoine's</option>
      </optgroup>
      <optgroup label="Cajun">
        <option value="bayoubobs">Bayou Bob's</option>
        <option value="pappadeaux" disabled="disabled">Pappadeaux</option>
        <option value="luciles">Lucile's</option>
      </optgroup>
    </select>
  </div>
</form>
<div data-role="controlgroup" data-type="horizontal">
  <a href="#" data-role="button">Yes</a>
  <a href="#" data-role="button">No</a>
  <a href="#" data-role="button">Cancel</a>
</div>
  </div>
  </div>
  <footer data-role="footer"><h1>O'Reilly</h1></footer>
</section>
```

Figure 4-1. Default swatch

Figure 4-2. Swatch A

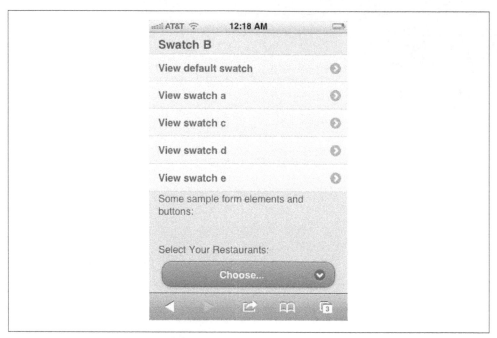

Figure 4-3. Swatch B

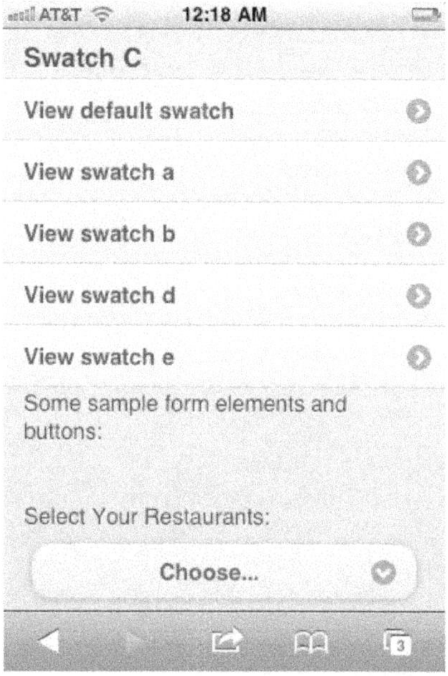

Figure 4-4. Swatch C

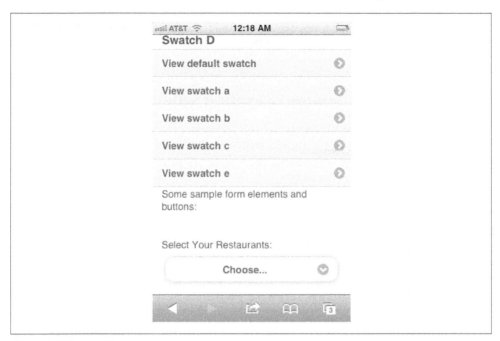

Figure 4-5. Swatch D

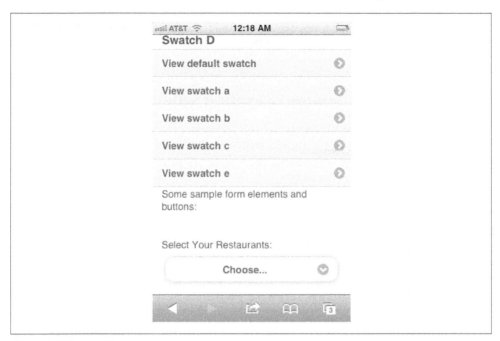

Figure 4-6. Swatch E

You can even mix and match swatches within a given page, giving you fine control over the look and feel of your application (Example 4-2).

Example 4-2. Mixing Swatches

```
<section id="swatch-mixed" data-role="page" data-theme="c">
  <header data-role="header" data-theme="b"><h1>jQuery Mobile</h1></header>
  <div class="content" data-role="content">
    <h3>Mixing Swatches</h3>
    <form  action="formprocessor.php" method="post">
      <div data-role="fieldcontain">
        <label for="select-restaurants">Select Your Restaurants:</label>
        <select id="select-restaurants"
                name="select-restaurants"
                data-native-menu="false"
                multiple="multiple"
                data-theme="e">
          <option value="choose" data-placeholder="true">Choose...</option>
          <optgroup label="French">
            <option value="lecentral">Le Central</option>
            <option value="bistrovandome">Bistro Vandome</option>
            <option value="antoines">Antoine's</option>
          </optgroup>
          <optgroup label="Cajun">
            <option value="bayoubobs">Bayou Bob's</option>
            <option value="pappadeaux" disabled="disabled">Pappadeaux</option>
            <option value="luciles">Lucile's</option>
          </optgroup>
        </select>
      </div>
    </form>
    <div data-role="controlgroup" data-type="horizontal">
      <a href="#" data-role="button" data-theme="a">Yes</a>
      <a href="#" data-role="button" data-theme="a">No</a>
      <a href="#" data-role="button" data-theme="a">Cancel</a>
    </div>
  </div>
  </div>
  <footer data-role="footer"><h1>O'Reilly</h1></footer>
</section>
```

Under The Hood: Customizing a Swatch

The theme swatches in jQuery Mobile are all defined by CSS, so they are easy to modify to suit your individual needs. The swatches are broken out into sections in the jQuery Mobile style sheet, and are straightforward.

The best way to modify a theme is to create a style sheet that overrides the desired styles and then load that style sheet after you load the jQuery Mobile style sheet. This is especially useful if you are using the CDN to serve the jQuery Mobile style sheet.

For example, let's say we want to change the yellow colors of Swatch E to be green. It's a simple matter of creating some override rules. In Example 4-3, I have copied and pasted the relevant rules from the Swatch E section of the jQuery Mobile style sheet and substituted my own colors.

Example 4-3. Override styles for Swatch E

```
/*
Change:
#fceda7 to #a7fcaf
#fadb4e to #5afa4e
#f7c942 to #5cf742
#33ff33 to #9efaa2
#fe3 to #33ff33
#fcf0b5 to #b5fcb5
#e79952 to #52e760
#fbe26f to #76fb6f
*/
.ui-bar-e {
    border: 1px solid        #5cf742;
    background:              #5afa4e;
    background-image: -moz-linear-gradient(top,
                             #a7fcaf,
                             #5afa4e);
    background-image: -webkit-gradient(linear,left top,left bottom,
        color-stop(0,        #a7fcaf),
        color-stop(1,        #5afa4e));
     -ms-filter: "progid:DXImageTransform.Microsoft.gradient(startColorStr='#a7fcaf',
        EndColorStr='#5afa4e')";
}
.ui-body-e {
    border: 1px solid        #5cf742;
    background:              #9efaa2;
    background-image: -moz-linear-gradient(top,
                             #fff,
                             #9efaa2);
    background-image: -webkit-gradient(linear,left top,left bottom,
        color-stop(0,        #fff),
        color-stop(1,        #9efaa2));
     -ms-filter: "progid:DXImageTransform.Microsoft.gradient(startColorStr='#ffffff',
        EndColorStr='#9efaa2')";
}
.ui-btn-up-e {
    border: 1px solid        #5cf742;
    background:              #5afa4e;
    text-shadow: 0 1px 1px       #33ff33;
    background-image: -moz-linear-gradient(top,
                             #a7fcaf,
                             #5afa4e);
    background-image: -webkit-gradient(linear,left top,left bottom,
        color-stop(0,        #a7fcaf),
        color-stop(1,        #5afa4e));
    -ms-filter: "progid:DXImageTransform.Microsoft.gradient(startColorStr='#a7fcaf',
        EndColorStr='#5afa4e')";
}

.ui-btn-hover-e {
```

```
    border: 1px solid          #52e760;
    background:                #76fb6f;
    background-image: -moz-linear-gradient(top,
                            #b5fcb5,
                            #76fb6f);
    background-image: -webkit-gradient(linear,left top,left bottom,
        color-stop(0,          #b5fcb5),
        color-stop(1,          #76fb6f));
    -ms-filter: "progid:DXImageTransform.Microsoft.gradient(startColorStr='#b5fcb5',
    EndColorStr='#76fb6f')";
}

.ui-btn-down-e {
    border: 1px solid          #5cf742;
    background:                #a7fcaf;
    background-image: -moz-linear-gradient(top,
                            #5afa4e,
                            #a7fcaf);
    background-image: -webkit-gradient(linear,left top,left bottom,
        color-stop(0,          #5afa4e),
        color-stop(1,          #a7fcaf));
    -ms-filter: "progid:DXImageTransform.Microsoft.gradient(startColorStr='#5afa4e',
    EndColorStr='#a7fcaf')";
}
```

If we load our new style sheet into a page set to use Swatch E (Example 4-4), we can
see the results (as illustrated in Figure 4-7).

Example 4-4. Swatch E goes green

```
<!DOCTYPE html>
<html>
  <head>
    <title>jQuery Mobile Application</title>

    <link rel="stylesheet" href="http://code.jquery.com/mobile/1.0a4.1/
    jquery.mobile-1.0a4.1.min.css" />
    <link rel="stylesheet" href="swatch-e-custom.css" />
    <script src="http://code.jquery.com/jquery-1.5.2.min.js"></script>
    <script src="http://code.jquery.com/mobile/1.0a4.1/jquery.mobile-1.0a4.1.min.js">
  </script>
  </head>

  <body>

    <section id="swatch-e" data-role="page" data-theme="e">
      <header data-role="header"><h1>Swatch E</h1></header>
      <div class="content" data-role="content">
        <h3>Swatch E: New and Improved</h3>
        <p>Some sample form elements and buttons:</p>
        <form  action="formprocessor.php" method="post">
          <div data-role="fieldcontain">
            <label for="select-restaurants">Select Your Restaurants:</label>
            <select id="select-restaurants"
                    name="select-restaurants"
```

```
                    data-native-menu="false"
                    multiple="multiple">
            <option value="choose" data-placeholder="true">Choose...</option>
            <optgroup label="French">
              <option value="lecentral">Le Central</option>
              <option value="bistrovandome">Bistro Vandome</option>
              <option value="antoines">Antoine's</option>
            </optgroup>
            <optgroup label="Cajun">
              <option value="bayoubobs">Bayou Bob's</option>
              <option value="pappadeaux" disabled="disabled">Pappadeaux</option>
              <option value="luciles">Lucile's</option>
            </optgroup>
          </select>
        </div>
      </form>
      <div data-role="controlgroup" data-type="horizontal">
        <a href="#" data-role="button">Yes</a>
        <a href="#" data-role="button">No</a>
        <a href="#" data-role="button">Cancel</a>
      </div>
    </div>
    <footer data-role="footer"><h1>jQuery Mobile</h1></footer>
  </section>

</body>
</html>
```

Note that I have included my custom Swatch E style sheet after the jQuery Mobile style sheet, thus guaranteeing that my styles will supersede the default styles.

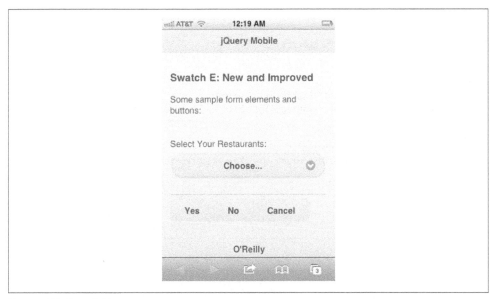

Figure 4-7. Swatch E goes green

Theming List View Elements

For added flexibility in list views, jQuery Mobile has implemented some specific data-attributes for theming dividers, count bubbles, and split buttons.

To theme a list divider, you can either apply a `data-theme` attribute to it directly, or you can use `data-divider-theme` attribute, which you can apply to the parent `ul` tag.

For count bubbles, use the `data-count-theme` attribute. You can apply it to the containing `ul` tag to theme all count bubbles in the list, or to individual list items to specify different count bubble themes within a given list.

Use the `data-split-theme` and `data-split-icon` attributes to theme split buttons. The `data-split-theme` attribute allows you to specify the theme of the right button in split buttons, and can be applied to either the containing `ul` or to individual list items.

To specify an icon for split buttons, use the `data-split-icon` attribute, as I have done in Example 4-5. This is most useful when specifying a default icon for all split buttons in a list view, rather than having to apply a `data-icon` attribute to each individual list item.

Example 4-5. Theming list view elements

```
<ul data-role="listview"
    data-split-icon="star"
    data-divider-theme="e"
    data-count-theme="a">
  <li data-role="list-divider">
    French Restaurants
    <span class="ui-li-count">3</span>
  </li>
  <li>
    <a href="lecentral.html">Le Central</a>
    <a href="reservations.php?restaurant=403">Make Reservations</a>
  </li>
  <li>
    <a href="bistrovandome.html">Bistro Vandome</a>
    <a href="reservations.php?restaurant=404">Make Reservations</a>
  </li>
  <li>
    <a href="antoines.html">Antoine's</a>
    <a href="reservations.php?restaurant=405">Make Reservations</a>
  </li>
</ul>
```

jQuery Mobile API

In addition to all of the predefined elements and interactions, jQuery Mobile exposes an extensive API consisting of methods, events, and configuration options. These give you finer control over jQuery Mobile elements and interactions.

jQuery Mobile Methods

jQuery Mobile provides a set of basic view-level methods. These methods enable you to manually handle pages and scrolling.

changePage

The `changePage` method is used to manually change views within a jQuery Mobile application. This is useful for programmatically changing pages in situations other than when the user simply taps on a link in the application.

As discussed in Chapter 2, jQuery Mobile updates the `location.hash` object as the user moves through pages in the application, allowing the framework to use the browser's native history capabilities to store the navigation information. The changePage method gives you an easy way to maintain that flexibility without having to manage the URLs yourself.

`changePage(` *to* `,` *transition* `,` *back* `,` *changeHash* `)`

- *to*: one of the following:
    - —a simple string denoting either an element ID or a filename
    - —an array of two elements, with the first being a simple string denoting the element ID or filename of the page to transition from, and the second being a simple string denoting the page to transition to
    - —an object with the following properties:
        - —*url*: the url string of the desired page
        - —*type*: the HTTP verb ("GET" or "POST")

—*data*: serialized parameters to send to the url

- *transition*: the name of the desired transition
- *back*: a Boolean indicating whether or not the transition should be in reverse
- *changeHash*: a Boolean indicating whether or not the `location.hash` should be updated upon successful transition

pageLoading

The `pageLoading` method shows and hides the jQuery Mobile loading dialog. Calling the method without a value shows the loading dialog. To hide the dialog again, call the method and pass a value of true (Example 5-1).

Example 5-1. Using the pageLoading method

```
<script>
// Show the page loading dialog
$.mobile.pageLoading();
// Asynchronously refresh the restaurant list
$.get("restaurant-list.html?type=french", function(strListHtml) {
  // Append the list to the DOM and make it a list view
  $(".container-restaurant-list").html(strListHtml).listview();
  // Hide the loading dialog
  $.mobile.pageLoading(true);
});
</script>
```

This method is particularly useful for providing feedback to the user that the application is busy. Just be sure to account for hiding the dialog under all conditions, including error conditions!

silentScroll

The `silentScroll` method gives you direct control over scrolling the content in the viewport. Calling this method does not trigger scroll event listeners.

The method takes an integer argument which corresponds to the y-position to scroll to (Example 5-2).

Example 5-2. Using the silentScroll Method

```
<script>
// Scroll down to the desired location
$.mobile.silentScroll(500);
</script>
```

addResolutionBreakpoints

See "Responsive Layout API" on page 85.

Events

jQuery Mobile includes a whole new set of events geared around mobile applications.

Touch Events

jQuery Mobile enables several new touch event categories:

tap
> A tap event, triggered when the user taps on an element

taphold
> A tap-and-hold event, triggered when the user taps and holds on an element for about a second

swipe
> A swipe event, triggered when the user swipes either vertically (20 or fewer pixels) or horizontally (30 or more pixels)

swipeleft
> A left-directed swipe, triggered when the user swipes to the left 30 or more pixels

swiperight
> A right-directed swipe, triggered when the user swipes to the right 30 or more pixels

All these events can be bound to elements using the usual jQuery bind, live, or delegate methods. Example 5-3 shows how to use these touch events.

Example 5-3. Using jQuery Mobile touch events

```
<script>
$("ul").delegate("li", "swiperight", function() {
  // The user has swiped to the right on a list view item.  Show an edit menu.
  $(this).find(".menu-edit").show();
})
</script>
```

Under The Hood: Using Swipe Events to Trigger Page Transitions

Using these new events, it's easy to set up an application that uses swipe events to trigger page transitions. Combined with the page transition features of jQuery Mobile, this can make for a powerful user experience.

As a simple example, let's add to our three-page example from Chapter 2, as I have done in Example 5-4.

Example 5-4. Simple application with three pages

```
<!-- begin first page -->
<section id="page1" data-role="page">
  <header data-role="header"><h1>jQuery Mobile</h1></header>
  <div  data-role="content" class="content">
    <p>First page!</p>
```

```
    </div>
    <footer data-role="footer"><h1>O'Reilly</h1></footer>
  </section>
  <!-- end first page -->

  <!-- Begin second page -->
  <section id="page2" data-role="page">
    <header data-role="header"><h1>jQuery Mobile</h1></header>
    <div data-role="content" class="content">
      <p>Second page!</p>
    </div>
    <footer data-role="footer"r><h1>O'Reilly</h1></footer>
  </section>
  <!-- end second page -->

  <!-- begin third page -->
  <section id="page3" data-role="page">
    <header data-role="header"><h1>jQuery Mobile</h1></header>
    <div data-role="content" class="content">
      <p>Third page!</p>
    </div>
    <footer data-role="footer"><h1>O'Reilly</h1></footer>
  </section>
  <!-- end third page -->
```

We want to make our new application respond to swipe events: swiping to the left should cause an animated transition to the next page, and swiping to the right should cause an animated transition to the previous page. All we have to do is attach swipe left and swiperight event listeners to each page, as in Example 5-5.

Example 5-5. Event handlers for swipe events

```
<script>
(function($) {
  var methods = {
    init : function(options) {
      var settings = {
        callback: function() {}
      };
      if ( options ) {
        $.extend( settings, options );
      }

      // Select all of the pages and then attach the event listeners
      $(":jqmData(role='page')").each(function() {
        $(this).bind("swipeleft", function() {

          // Get the current page number from the id and increment it by 1.
          var nextPage = parseInt($(this).attr("id").split("page")[1]) +1;
          if (nextPage === 4) nextPage = 1;

          // Transition the page.
          $.mobile.changePage("#page"+nextPage, "slide");

        });
```

```
        $(this).bind("swiperight", function() {

            // Get the current page number from the id and decrement it by 1.
            var nextPage = parseInt($(this).attr("id").split("page")[1]) -1;
            if (nextPage === 0) nextPage = 3;

            // Transition the page.
            $.mobile.changePage("#page"+nextPage, "slide", true);
          })
        })

      }
    }

    $.fn.initApp = function(method) {
      // Method calling logic
      if ( methods[method] ) {
        return methods[method].apply(this, Array.prototype.slice.call(arguments, 1));
      } else if ( typeof method === 'object' || ! method ) {
        return methods.init.apply( this, arguments );
      } else {
        $.error( 'Method ' + method + ' does not exist' );
      }
    }
})(jQuery);

$(document).ready(function() {
  $().initApp();
})
</script>
```

Here I have used the jQuery plug-in pattern (just copied and pasted directly from the documentation) to create a quick application initialization plug-in. I then call that plug-in on document ready.

The result is an application that responds to swipe events in either direction and transitions to the appropriate page.

Initialization Events

As jQuery Mobile initializes a page view (an element with a data-role="page"), it fires off the pagebeforecreate event (before a page is initialized) and pagecreate (after a page is initialized). Since page initialization only happens once, these events only fire once for a given page (unlike page hide and show events, which fire every time a transition happens).

These events can be bound to the page element itself (Example 5-6).

Example 5-6. Using the page initialization events

```
// Bind to the pagebeforecreate event for all pages
$('section[data-role="page"]').live("pagebeforecreate", function() {
  // Asynchronously include a footer template
  var $this = $(this);
  $.get("templates/footer.html", function(strFooterHtml) {
      $this.append(strFooterHtml);
  })
})

// Bind a scroll event listener to the long scrolling page
$("#restaurantListPage").live("pagecreate", function() {
  $(this).bind("scrollstop", function() {
    // Show the "back to top" button at the correct position
    showBackToTop();
  })
})
```

 You can prevent jQuery Mobile from initializing a page entirely if you return *false* from its pagebeforecreate event handler.

Page Hide and Show Events

As jQuery Mobile hides and shows pages, it fires off events before and afterwards on both the page being hidden and the page being shown. jQuery Mobile provides four such events, each of which provides a reference to the event and ui objects:

pagebeforehide
> This event fires on the page being transitioned from, before the transition between pages starts. ui.nextPage will be either the page being transitioned to, or an empty jQuery object if there is none.

pagebeforeshow
> This event fires on the page being transitioned to, before the transition between pages starts. ui.prevPage will be the page being transitioned from, or an empty jQuery object if there is none.

pagehide
> This event fires on the page being transitioned from, after the transition finishes. ui.nextPage will be the jQuery object of the page being transitioned to, or empty if it does not exist.

pageshow
> This event fires on the page being transitioned to, after the transition finishes. ui.prevPage will contain the jQuery object of the page being transitioned from, or empty if it does not exist.

Scroll Events

In addition to the regular `scroll` event, jQuery Mobile makes the `scrollstart` and `scrollstop` events available for binding onto scrolling elements. These can be particularly useful on long list views, allowing you to apply pre or post processing to elements as they come into and out of view.

 Beware: mobile scrolling is different than desktop scrolling. Mobile scrolling is usually eased, meaning it gradually slows down over time before coming to a complete stop (and thus firing `scrollstop`). Also, sometimes users come to "rolling stops" as they scroll through content: they don't actually stop completely, but rather flick through a long page and just as the animation is about to end, they scroll again. This can prevent the expected events from firing at all, or make them fire only once.

Orientation Change Events

If the orientation of the device changes, jQuery Mobile will fire off an `orientation change` event. The event will have as an argument the *orientation* property, which will be set to either *portrait* or *landscape*. This provides a programmatic way of handling orientation changes in addition to using CSS selectors. For detailed information, see "Responsive Layout API" on page 85.

Responsive Layout API

Mobile devices come in many screen widths and resolutions, and people can use them in portrait or landscape mode. jQuery Mobile provides a responsive layout framework for handling these situations, enabling you to build mobile application interfaces that have the benefits of both fluid and fixed layouts.

The responsive layout framework consists of CSS selectors built around device orientation and screen size, orientation change events, and dynamic media queries.

CSS Selectors

jQuery Mobile will attach various CSS classes to the HTML element depending on the current orientation of the device and size of the viewport. These classes are automatically updated whenever a load, resize, or orientation change event occurs.

If the device is in landscape mode, jQuery Mobile will apply a `.landscape` class to the HTML element. Likewise, if the device is in portrait mode, jQuery Mobile will apply a `.portrait` class to the HTML element. You can use these selectors within your own CSS to create layouts that alter themselves to respond to device orientation.

For example, let's say you want to change the background of the application depending on the orientation of the device. In portrait mode you want to have an image, but if the device is in landscape mode you just want a simple background gradient. To achieve this, all you need to do is write a couple of CSS rules that cascade off of the `.portrait` and `.landscape` classes (Example 5-7).

Example 5-7. Using the jQuery Mobile orientation classes

```
.portrait section {
  background-image: url(images/portrait-background.png);
}

.landscape section {
  background: #9efaa2;
  background-image: -moz-linear-gradient(top, #fff, #9efaa2);
  background-image: -webkit-gradient(linear,left top,left bottom,
                    color-stop(0, #fff),
                    color-stop(1, #9efaa2));
  -ms-filter: "progid:DXImageTransform.Microsoft.gradient(startColorStr='#ffffff',
              EndColorStr='#9efaa2')";
}
```

In this example, each section tag will have either a background image (if the device is in portrait mode) or a green gradient (if the device is in landscape mode).

Screen Size Breakpoint Classes

In addition to orientation changes, jQuery Mobile provides a way to handle different screen sizes with CSS classes that are based on the size of the screen. jQuery Mobile refers to these as "breakpoint classes." The default screen size breakpoints for jQuery Mobile are 320 pixels, 480 pixels, 768 pixels, and 1024 pixels. These in turn translate into min-width and max-width CSS classes: `min-width-320px`, `max-width-768px`, etc. As with the orientation classes, jQuery Mobile applies these breakpoint classes to the HTML element.

Returning to our previous example, let's say you want to have a different background image depending on the resolution of the screen (Example 5-8).

Example 5-8. CSS snippet demonstrating breakpoint classes

```
/* Show a different background image depending on screen resolution */
#pageLogin {
  background-color: #ccc;
}
.min-width-320px #pageLogin,
.max-width-480px #pageLogin {
  background-image: url(images/login-bg-320.jpg);
}

.min-width-480px #pageLogin,
.max-width-768px #pageLogin {
  background-image: url(images/login-bg-480.jpg);
```

```
}

.min-width-768px #pageLogin,
.max-width-1024px #pageLogin {
  background: #9efaa2;
  background-image: -moz-linear-gradient(top, #fff, #9efaa2);
  background-image: -webkit-gradient(linear,left top,left bottom,
                    color-stop(0, #fff),
                    color-stop(1, #9efaa2));
  -ms-filter: "progid:DXImageTransform.Microsoft.gradient(startColorStr='#ffffff',
              EndColorStr='#9efaa2')";
}
```

Here, you will see one image if your screen resolution is between 320 and 480 pixels wide, another image if it is between 480 and 768 pixels wide, and a green gradient if the screen size is any larger.

Adding Size Breakpoints. Don't like jQuery Mobile's default size breakpoints? You can add your own using the `addResolutionBreakpoints` method, as I have done in Example 5-9. The `addResolutionBreakpoints` method takes as an argument an integer (corresponding to a resolution breakpoint) or array of integers (each corresponding to a resolution breakpoint), and jQuery Mobile will automatically apply the appropriate classes to the HTML element.

Example 5-9. Adding screen size breakpoints

```
// The restaurant list page is particularly complex and needs extra
// breakpoints
$("#restaurantListPage").live("pagecreate", function() {
  $.mobile.addResolutionBreakpoints([400, 600]);
})
```

Orientation Change Events

In addition to automatically applying CSS classes to the HTML tag, jQuery Mobile also fires off an `orientationchange` events whenever the user changes the orientation of the device. The `orientationchange` event will pass into its listener an *orientation* property that will be set to either *portrait* or *landscape*.

Using this event you can create even more dynamic layouts than you could with just CSS selectors alone. You can programmatically alter your layouts, or even load different content for different orientations (Example 5-10).

Example 5-10. Using the orientationchange event

```
<script>
$("#page1").bind("orientationchange", function(orientation) {
    // Show the loading dialog
    $.mobile.pageLoading();

    // dynamically load different content depending on orientation
    if (orientation === "landscape") {
```

```
            $("#content").load("pageone-landscape.html");
    } else if (orientation === "portrait") {
            $("#content").load("pageone-portrait.html");
    } else {
            $("#content").load("pageone-desktop.html");
    }
})
</script>
```

Media Queries

Finally, jQuery Mobile has the `media` method for making direct media queries. The method takes any standard CSS Media Query as an argument, and if the browser supports the media type and if it is currently active, the method will return true. This can be useful for determining certain details about the device, such as whether or not it has a retina display (Example 5-11).

Example 5-11. Using a media query

```
<script>
var boolRetina = $.mobile.media("-webkit-min-device-pixel-ratio: 2");
if (boolRetina) {
  $("#content").css("background-image","url('images/bg-retina.png')");
}
</script>
```

 What's a media query? You are probably familiar with specifying a `media` attribute on CSS link tags (e.g., `media="screen"` or `media="print"`). The CSS 3 specification expands these media types significantly. See the Media Query specification at *http://www.w3.org/ TR/css3-mediaqueries/*. Media queries are simply determining whether or not a particular media type is both supported by the browser and is in effect.

Configuring jQuery Mobile

jQuery Mobile has several configuration options that you can set that will alter its behavior across all pages.

Available Options

string `activeBtnClass`
    The CSS class applied to active buttons. Default: "ui-btn-active".

string `activePageClass`
    The CSS class applied to the page that is currently visible. Default: "ui-page-active".

boolean `ajaxEnabled`

Enable or disable asynchronous features: ajax form handling, ajax link handling, and URL hash management. Setting this to false will disable all three features. Defaults to true.

boolean `ajaxFormsEnabled`

Enable or disable asynchronous form handling. Defaults to true.

boolean `ajaxLinksEnabled`

Enable or disable asynchronous link handling. Defaults to true.

string `defaultTransition`

The default transition animation to show when transitioning between pages. Defaults to "slide".

boolean `hashListeningEnabled`

Enable or disable hash management. Defaults to true.

`gradeA`

jQuery Mobile extends the base `jQuery.support` object with a new property: `media query`. `gradeA` is an alias to that property. This gives you fine control over required features that must be in place for your application to function. To use this property, define a function that detects the feature in question and returns either true or false (see Example 5-13).

string `loadingMessage`

The string to display in the loading indicator dialog. Defaults to "Loading".

string `nonHistorySelectors`

If a page has a `data-rel` or `data-role` set to one of these selectors, it will not be included in the URL history hash. Defaults to "dialog".

string `ns`

A default namespace to apply to the custom `data-` attributes, e.g. setting this to "foo-" will make jQuery Mobile only look for `data-foo-` attributes: `data-foo-role,` `data-foo-transition`, etc. Defaults to "".

string `pageLoadErrorMessage`

The string to display when jQuery Mobile fails to load a page. Defaults to "Error Loading Page".

string `subPageUrlKey`

The string to use in the URL to reference a sub-page, e.g. *http://www.site.com/ index.html&ui-page=#page1*. Defaults to "ui-page".

Changing an Option via mobileinit

Each of these options is a property on the `$.mobile` object: `$.mobile.defaultTransition = "flip"` or `$.mobile.loadingMessage = "Please Wait..."` Simply apply the new values you want to use.

To set these options, you will need to bind to the `mobileinit` event. As jQuery Mobile begins its execution, it fires off the `mobileinit` event and you can bind to it like any other event. However, `mobileinit` happens as jQuery Mobile is loaded, so if you want to bind to it you will need to load your event handler script before you load jQuery Mobile (Example 5-12).

Example 5-12. Loading a configuration script

```
<script src="http://code.jquery.com/jquery-1.5.2.min.js"></script>
<script src="jquery-mobile-defaults.js"></script>
<script src="http://code.jquery.com/mobile/1.0a4.1/jquery.mobile-1.0a4.1.min.js"></script>
```

Here we are including a new script file, `jquery-mobile-defaults.js`, which will execute before jQuery Mobile and contains the `mobileinit` event handler shown in Example 5-13.

Example 5-13. Setting jQuery Mobile defaults

```
<script>
$(document).bind("mobileinit", function() {
  $.extend(  $.mobile , {
    defaultTransition : "flip",
    loadingMessage : "Please Wait...",
    gradeA: function() {
      // Our application should only work in browsers that support
      // CSS transitions.
      var div = document.createElement('div');
      div.innerHTML = '<div style="-webkit-transition:color 1s linear;
                                    -moz-transition:color 1s linear;"></div>';
      var cssTransitionsSupported = false;
      cssTransitionsSupported =
        (div.firstChild.style.webkitTransition !== undefined) ||
        (div.firstChild.style.MozTransition !== undefined);
      return cssTransitionsSupported;
    }
  });
})
</script>
```

In this example, we are setting the default page transition to "flip" and the loading message to "Please Wait..." In addition, we are detecting whether or not the browser supports CSS transitions, and requiring that via gradeA. In browsers that do not support CSS transitions, jQuery Mobile will not initialize.

Under The Hood: Namespacing Data Attributes

As mentioned in Chapter 1, jQuery Mobile relies heavily on data- attributes. Because of this, it might make sense for you to namespace your jQuery Mobile-specific data-attributes to distinguish them from other data- attributes that you might be using in your application. For example, instead of using data-role="page" you might want to use data-jqm-role="page".

Through the `$.mobile.ns` configuration option, you can easily set jQuery Mobile up to handle namespaces (Example 5-14).

Example 5-14. Configuring jQuery Mobile to use a namespace

```
<script>
$(document).bind("mobileinit", function() {
  $.extend( $.mobile , {
    ns : "jqm-"
  });
})
</script>
```

You can still easily select your namespaced `data-` attributes using the `jqmData()` selector, which automatically accounts for the namespace you define in the `$.mobile.ns` property. `$(":jqmData(role='page')")` will select all of the elements in your application with the `data-jqm-role="header"` attribute.

jQuery Mobile in Action

Putting this all together, we are ready to build an actual mobile application with jQuery Mobile. Let's start with a simple mobile Twitter client: jqmTweet. jqmTweet will have the following features:

- Display the first page of tweets of the desired Twitter user in a list view
- Tapping on a tweet will display a detail page for that tweet
- The Twitter user and number of tweets to display needs to be configurable
- The application must handle errors gracefully

Application Pages

One of the best ways to approach a new jQuery Mobile application is to think of it in terms of individual pages. Because it's so easy to create individual pages in jQuery Mobile, it often makes sense to build out all of the pages with placeholder text that you can fill in with data later. In addition to getting you up and running quickly, it also provides the potential benefit of creating an interactive prototype that you can use for demonstrations or user testing. Need to get stakeholder buy-in for the new application? Want to do some feature validation with your users? No problem, just mock out your application pages in jQuery Mobile.

For jqmTweet, the application will have a main page (with the list of tweets), a detail page (for displaying the details of an individual tweet), a configuration page (for updating the Twitter user name and number of tweets), and an error page (for error dialogs).

First off, the main page will look as shown in Example 6-1.

Example 6-1. jqmTweet main tweet list view

```
<!-- Begin: Main tweet list view -->
<section id="pageTweetList" data-role="page">
  <header data-role="header" data-position="fixed">
    <h1>jqmTweet</h1>
```

```
  <a href="#pageSettings"
     data-transition="flip"
     data-role="button"
     data-icon="gear"
     data-iconpos="notext"
     class="ui-btn-right">Options</a>
  </header>
  <div class="content" data-role="content">
    <ul data-role="listview">
      <li><a href="#pageTweetDetail">Tweet!</a></li>
      <li><a href="#pageTweetDetail">Tweet!</a></li>
      <li><a href="#pageTweetDetail">Tweet!</a></li>
      <li><a href="#pageTweetDetail">Tweet!</a></li>
      <li><a href="#pageTweetDetail">Tweet!</a></li>
      <li><a href="#pageTweetDetail">Tweet!</a></li>
      <li><a href="#pageTweetDetail">Tweet!</a></li>
      <li><a href="#pageTweetDetail">Tweet!</a></li>
    </ul>
  </div>
  <footer data-role="footer" data-position="fixed"><h1>O'Reilly <i>jQuery Mobile</i></h1></footer>
</section>
<!-- End: Main tweet list view -->
```

There's a header and a footer, and a list view in the content area. In the header, a button links off to the settings page, and we have defined the appearance of the button specified in the transition between the main page and the settings page. The settings page will look as shown in Example 6-2.

Example 6-2. jqmTweet settings page

```
<!-- Begin: Settings page -->
<section id="pageSettings" data-role="page">
  <header data-role="header"><h1>jqmTweet</h1></header>
  <div class="content" data-role="content">
    <h3>Settings</h3>
    <div data-role="fieldcontain">
      <label for="username">Twitter User Name:</label>
      <input type="text" id="username" value="">
    </div>
    <div data-role="fieldcontain">
      <label for="slider">Number of tweets to display:</label>
      <input type="range" id="slider" name="slider" min="5" max="50" value="">
    </div>
  </div>
  <footer data-role="footer"><h1>O'Reilly <i>jQuery Mobile</i></h1></footer>
</section>
<!-- End: Preferences page -->
```

Here we have an input field for the Twitter user name and a slider for changing the desired number of tweets.

A tweet detail page will be very easy (Example 6-3).

Example 6-3. jqmTweet tweet detail page

```
<!-- Begin: Tweet detail view -->
<section id="pageTweetDetail" data-role="page">
  <header data-role="header"><h1>jqmTweet</h1></header>
  <div class="content" data-role="content">
    <div class="container-tweet">
        <p>Tweet!</p>
    </div>
  </div>
  <footer data-role="footer"><h1>O'Reilly <i>jQuery Mobile</i></h1></footer>
</section>
<!-- End: Tweet detail view -->
```

And the error dialog page will be similarly simple (Example 6-4).

Example 6-4. jqmTweet error dialog page

```
<!-- Begin: Error page -->
<section id="pageError" data-role="page" data-theme="e">
  <header data-role="header"><h1>jqmTweet</h1></header>
  <div class="content" data-role="content">
  </div>
  <footer data-role="footer"><h1>O'Reilly <i>jQuery Mobile</i></h1></footer>
</section>
<!-- End: Error page -->
```

Here I've specified Swatch E for the theme. The basic views that we will use to display
the information from the Twitter API are shown in Figures 6-1, 6-2, and 6-3.

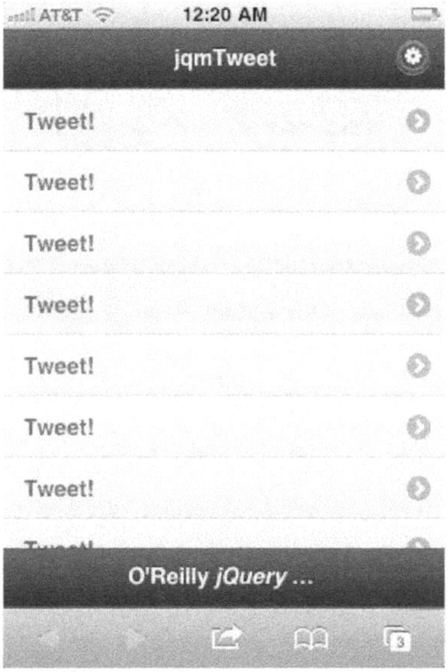

Figure 6-1. jqmTweet: Tweet list page

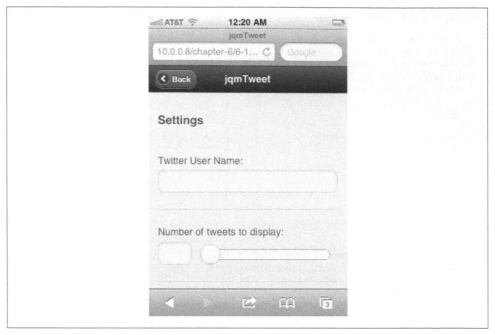

Figure 6-2. jqmTweet: Settings page

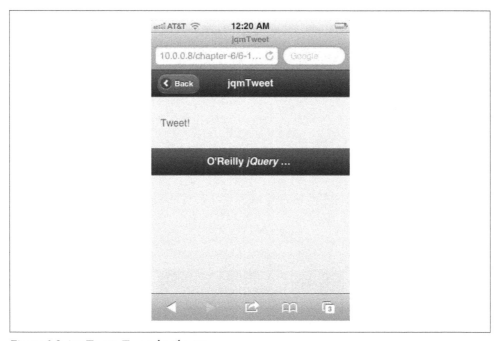

Figure 6-3. jqmTweet: Tweet detail page

Initializing the Application

Now that we have the individual pages in place, we can start thinking about filling them in with data. It's useful to wrap application initialization in a jQuery plug-in that initializes each page in a different method. Here's the basic pattern, applied to jqmTweet:

```
(function($) {
  var methods = {
    initMainPage : function() {
    },

    initDetailPage : function() {
    },

    initSettingsPage : function() {
    },

    initAll : function() {
      $().initApp("initMainPage");
      $().initApp("initDetailPage");
      $().initApp("initSettingsPage");
    }
  }

  $.fn.initApp = function(method) {
    // Method calling logic
    if ( methods[method] ) {
      return methods[ method ].apply( this,
      Array.prototype.slice.call( arguments, 1 ));
    } else if ( typeof method === 'object' || ! method ) {
      return methods.initAll.apply( this, arguments );
    } else {
      $.error( 'Method ' + method + ' does not exist' );
    }
  }
})(jQuery);
```

Then on document ready we can just call the new `jQuery.initApp()` function and everything will be initialized.

 This is almost a straight up copy-and-paste of the jQuery plug-in pattern. I've left out the options since we don't need them, and I've altered method calling logic so that `initAll` is the default method for the plug-in, but otherwise it's the same. The jQuery plug-in pattern is very useful; if you don't already know about it, you can read more on the jQuery documentation site at *http://docs.jquery.com/Plugins/Authoring*.

The initMainPage Method

We'll start with the main page. The main page needs to display the Twitter feed when the app first loads, and it needs to refresh the feed if the user changes something on the settings page. So we'll need a way of accessing the Twitter API and translating the data into HTML that we can use in a jQuery Mobile listview.

Under The Hood: Passing Data Between jQuery Mobile Pages

Our application will need to communicate between pages: the main page will need to know what parameters (if any) were changed on the settings page, and the tweet detail page will need to know what specific tweet to display.

In traditional web applications, passing information between separate pages required something like cookies. But since the pages in a jQuery Mobile application all exist within the same DOM, there are a few more techniques available:

HTML 5 DOM storage
> You can use the HTML 5 `sessionStorage` or `localStorage` methods. This choice leads in nicely to caching information even when the user ends their session. These features are also widely supported in mobile browsers.

Global variables
> Since all of the pages are in one DOM, you can easily use global variables to transmit information from one page to another. One page sets a variable, and when the next page loads, it checks the same variable and retrieves the information. Global variables are generally frowned upon as bad development practice, but if you namespace the variables appropriately, it can be a quick, effective method to use.

The `jQuery.data()` method
> You can store data directly in DOM elements using the `jQuery.data()` method. You can read more about the `jQuery.data()` method in the jQuery documentation, but basically it allows you to attach key-value pairs to any DOM element. Since all the pages in a jQuery Mobile application are in the same DOM, any page can access the data attached to any element.

We'll use `jQuery.data()` to store information that each page needs to know. The main page will need to know the Twitter user name to search for and how many tweets to retrieve, so we'll store that information on that page.

Now back to getting the data from Twitter.

Accessing the Twitter API

Twitter provides a simple RESTful API for fetching tweets. Basically, you send a simple HTTP GET request to search.twitter.com with some URL parameters, and it will respond with either the requested data or error information. Using the URL parameters, you can specify how many tweets to fetch on the first page, what user you want to search for, and the format of the returned data (JSON or XML).

JSON or XML? Because we're doing everything in JavaScript, JSON is a logical choice for our data format. Though jQuery has a build-in JSON parsing function (which takes a JSON string and returns the equivalent object), it does not (yet) have a built-in JSON serializing function (which takes a JSON object and returns a properly formatted string). Because of this, we'll be using Crockford's JSON.js library, available at *https://github.com/douglascrockford/JSON-js*. Crockford's library is lightweight and simple to use, and is ideal for our situation. It has two methods: `JSON.parse()` (which takes a JSON-formatted string and returns an object) and `JSON.stringify()` (which takes an object and returns a JSON-formatted string).

 JSON stands for "JavaScript Object Notation" and is a specification for representing JavaScript objects as formatted strings. If you're not familiar with JSON, you can read about it at *http://www.json.org/*, where there are many resources, tutorials, and examples.

Fetching the Data. To get the data from the Twitter API, we can use the `jQuery.ajax()` method. If you've never used this, you can read more about it in the documentation, but basically it provides a cross-browser AJAX implementation. Here's the basic call:

```
$.ajax({
  url: 'http://search.twitter.com/search.json?rpp=20&q=from:jreid01',
  dataType: 'json',
  success: function(data) {
  },
  error: function() {
  }
});
```

This will query search.twitter.com and ask for the first twenty tweets from user jreid01 to be returned in JSON format. Once the query is done and the service responds, either the error function will be triggered (if something went wrong) or the success function will be triggered.

The success function will receive the JSON data object for it to process. The object will consist of an array called "results" and each item in the array will be an object that will look something like this:

```
{"from_user_id_str":"33001383",
 "profile_image_url":"http://a1.twimg.com/profile_images/347035711/me_normal.jpg",
 "created_at":"Fri, 13 May 2011 15:43:18 +0000",
 "from_user":"jreid01",
 "id_str":"69065189441544192",
 "metadata":{"result_type":"recent"},
 "to_user_id":null,
 "text":"Anatidaephobia: the fear that somewhere, somehow,
 a duck is watching you. #lesserknownphobias",
 "id":69065189441544192,
 "from_user_id":33001383,
 "geo":null,
 "iso_language_code":"en",
 "to_user_id_str":null,
 "source":"&lt;a href=&quot;http://www.tweetdeck.com&quot;
 rel=&quot;nofollow&quot;&gt;TweetDeck&lt;/a&gt;"}
```

The value of each property will change for each item, but the schema will be the same for all items. There's a lot of useful information in each result object, including the profile image URL and the text of the tweet.

We can easily loop through the results array and extract the information we need, and use it to build the HTML for our list view. Then we can append the new list to the DOM and call jQuery Mobile's `listview` widget. A function to do all of this is shown in Example 6-5.

Example 6-5. jqmTweet's updateTwitterFeed function

```
var updateTwitterFeed = function() {

  // Get the page and list we need to work with
  var $page = $("#pageTweetList");

  // Build the URL we need using the data stored on the main view page
  var strUrl = "http://search.twitter.com/search.json?callback=?&rpp=";
  strUrl += $page.data("rpp");
  strUrl += "&q=from:" + $page.data("twitterUser");

  // Get the tweets and append them to the list
  $.ajax({
    url: strUrl,
    dataType: 'json',
    success: function(data) {

      // Delete the existing list, if any
      $page.find(".content").empty();

      // Create a new list
      $page.find(".content").html("<ul></ul>");
      $list = $page.find(".content ul");

      for (var i = 0; i < data.results.length; i++) {

        // Build HTML that contains the desired information
        var strHtml = '<li><a href="#pageTweetDetail">';
        strHtml += '<img src="'+data.results[i].profile_image_url+'">';
        strHtml += data.results[i].text;
        strHtml += '</a></li>\n';

        // Make it into a jQuery object...
        var tweet = $(strHtml);

        // ...so we can append it to our list.
        $list.append(tweet);

        // Store the JSON data for this tweet (we will
        // need it for the detail page)
        $list.find("a:last").data("tweetJSON", JSON.stringify(data.results[i]));
      }

      // Call the listview widget.
```

```
      $list.listview();

      // When the user taps on a tweet, it will go to the detail page.
      // We need to give the detail page the data it needs to display.
      $list.find("a").click(function() {
        var $this = $(this);
        // Pass the tweetJSON object over to the detail page so that it
        // has the information it needs
        $("#pageTweetDetail").data("tweetJSON", $this.data("tweetJSON"));
      })
    },
    error: function() {
      alert("An error occurred. Please try again. ");
    }
  });
}
```

This function sends a GET request to the Twitter API, processes the response, and creates a list view. It also handles errors, though not very gracefully.

It also sets up a click listener on each list item, so that when the user taps an item to go to the detail page, the data on the detail page is updated with the information it needs to display.

Now our `initMainPage` method will look something like this:

```
initMainPage : function() {

  var $page = $("#pageTweetList");

  // Set some defaults
  $page.data("rpp", 20);
  $page.data("twitterUser", "jreid01");
  $page.data("boolUpdate", false);

  // Update the twitter feed for the first time
  updateTwitterFeed();

  // Every time we show this page we need to check to see if we need to update.
  $page.bind("pageshow", function(event, ui) {
    if ($page.data("boolUpdate")) {
      updateTwitterFeed();

      // And if we have updated, we need to reset the flag
      $page.data("boolUpdate", false);
    }
  })
}
```

The initSettings Method

The settings page needs to be initialized too. It needs to show the correct data, and if the user changes something, it needs to update that data in the main page, and set the update flag so the main page knows to update the feed when the user transitions back to it. It looks as shown in Example 6-6.

Example 6-6. jqmTweet initSettings method

```
initSettingsPage : function() {

  // Current page
  var $page = $("#pageSettings");
  // Page where data is stored
  var $datapage = $("#pageTweetList");

  // If the user changes the username we need
  // to update the data stored in $datapage
  $page.find("#username").change(function() {
    var newVal = $(this).val();
    $datapage.data("twitterUser", newVal);
    // Set the refresh boolean
    $datapage.data("boolUpdate", true);
  });

  // TRICK: jQuery Mobile doesn't have a change() event
  // for the slider yet, so we need to check it
  // when the user leaves this page
  $page.bind("pagebeforehide", function(event, ui) {
    var sliderValue = $page.find("#slider").val();
    // Has the value changed?
    if (parseInt(sliderValue, 10) != parseInt($datapage.data("rpp"), 10)) {
      // Yes it has, so update the data and set for refresh
      $datapage.data("rpp", sliderValue);
      $datapage.data("boolUpdate", true);
    }
  })

  // On page show we need to update the elements on
  // this page to reflect current data
  $page.bind("pageshow", function(event, ui) {
    $page.find("#slider").val($datapage.data("rpp")).slider("refresh");
    $page.find("#username").val($datapage.data("twitterUser"));
  })

}
```

The initDetailPage Method

The tweet detail page needs to display the tweet data. The only time we'll get to the detail page is if the user has tapped on a tweet in the main page list view, and each tweet in the list view has an event listener attached to it that will update the data attached to the detail page. So all we have to do is get the data that is attached to the page and display it. The resulting method is simple (Example 6-7).

Example 6-7. jqmTweet initDetailPage method

```
initDetailPage : function() {

  var $page = $("#pageTweetDetail");

  // Every time this page shows, we need to display a tweet detail
  $page.bind("pageshow", function(event, ui) {
    var objTweet = JSON.parse($page.data("tweetJSON"));
    var strHtml = '<p><img src="'+objTweet.profile_image_url+'">';
    strHtml += objTweet.text + '</p>';
    $page.find(".container-tweet").html(strHtml);
  });
}
```

That's it. jQuery Mobile will automatically give us a back button to return to the list view, so we don't have to do anything else.

Error Dialog

Finally, let's look at using the error dialog page we created. It doesn't need to be initialized, instead we'll be updating it with whatever error message we want and then manually showing it when we need to.

You can use the `$.mobile.changePage()` method to show a dialog, but an easier method is to place a button somewhere in the application (it doesn't even need to be in a page) and then hide it using CSS:

```
<a href="#pageError"
    id="show-error-page"
    data-role="button"
    data-rel="dialog"
    data-transition="pop"
    style="display: none">Show error page</a>
```

Whenever you need to show the error dialog, just update the content in the dialog and then trigger the button's click event with JavaScript. jQuery Mobile will handle everything for you.

If we use this technique, our `error` function in the `$.ajax()` call in the `updateTwitter` Feed function becomes:

```
error: function() {
  // Get the page
  var $page = $("#pageError .content");

  // Build an error message
  var strHtml = "<h3>Update failed</h3>";
  strHtml += "<p>We were unable to update the twitter feed.  Please try again.</p>"

  // Place the message in the error dialog
  $page.html(strHtml);

  // Show the dialog
  $("#show-error-page").click();
}
```

jqmTweet Take One

If we run the application as it stands, it works well. It displays the list of tweets, the user can change the number of tweets or the Twitter user to search for, and display the detail of any tweet (see Figures 6-4, 6-5, and 6-6).

It's a bare-bones client with few features, but it's solid.

Figure 6-4. jqmTweet: Live tweet list page

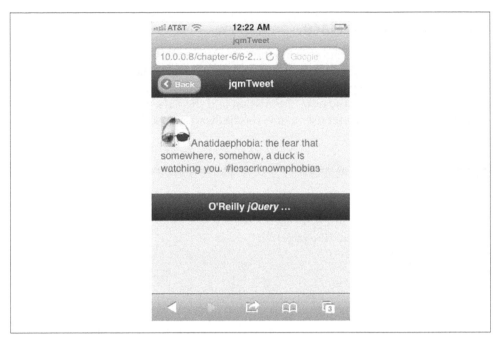

Figure 6-5. jqmTweet: Tweet detail page

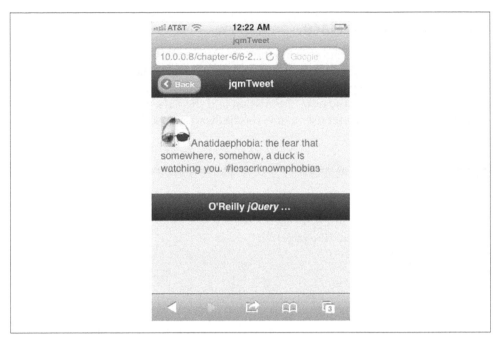

Figure 6-6. jqmTweet: Live settings page

Improving the Interface

Out of the box, the application works fine, but there are some problems. First, you can't read an entire tweet on the list page. And if you change the Twitter user name on the settings page, when you return to the list page, the application appears to "freeze" while it goes and fetches the new information and displays it for the user. And if the user enters an invalid Twitter user name, the application just displays a blank page for the list view.

CSS Tweaks

By default, jQuery Mobile truncates list view items to display only one line with an ellipsis. To do so, it uses this simple CSS rule:

```
.ui-li .ui-btn-text a.ui-link-inherit {
  text-overflow: ellipsis;
  overflow: hidden;
  white-space: nowrap;
}
```

This tells all anchor tags to not wrap their content, to hide any overflowing content, and to truncate it with an ellipsis. We'll need to override this for our application, and to do so we'll add a new style sheet that loads after the jQuery Mobile style sheet and has the following rule:

```
.ui-li .ui-btn-text a.ui-link-inherit {
  white-space: normal;
  padding-left: 60px;
}
```

This rule overrides the white-space rule of the default jQuery Mobile style sheet and will allow all of the tweet to display and wrap on the screen. In addition, we've altered the padding of the anchor tag so that it is closer to the Twitter user icon.

The Twitter user icon needs to have its margins tweaked as well, to better arrange it with the tweet text:

```
.ui-li-thumb {
    margin-top: 10px;
    margin-left: 10px;
}
```

This will just bump the Twitter user icon down a bit, putting it in better alignment with the tweet text.

Interaction Tweaks

If you change the number of tweets, or change the Twitter user to search for, when you return to the main page there's a lag as the application fetches the new information and then displays it. A big improvement would be to let the user know that something's happening, and jQuery Mobile's loading dialog is the perfect tool.

You can call the loading dialog manually using $.mobile.pageloading(), and then hide it again using $.mobile.pageloading(true). In our case, we'll want to do that in the updateTwitterFeed() function, which will now look as shown in Example 6-8.

Example 6-8. New and improved updateTwitterFeed function

```
var updateTwitterFeed = function() {
  // First, call the page loading dialog
  $.mobile.pageLoading();

  // Get the page and list we need to work with
  var $page = $("#pageTweetList");

  // Build the URL we need
  var strUrl = "http://search.twitter.com/search.json?callback=?&rpp=";
  strUrl += $page.data("rpp");
  strUrl += "&q=from:" + $page.data("twitterUser");

  // Get the tweets and append them to the list
  $.ajax({
    url: strUrl,
    dataType: 'json',
    success: function(data) {

      // Delete the existing list, if any
      $page.find(".content").empty();

      // Create a new list
      $page.find(".content").html("<ul></ul>");
      $list = $page.find(".content ul");

      for (var i = 0; i < data.results.length; i++) {

        // Build HTML that contains the desired information
        var strHtml = '<li><a href="#pageTweetDetail">';
        strHtml += '<img src="'+data.results[i].profile_image_url+'">';
        strHtml += data.results[i].text;
        strHtml += '</a></li>\n';

        // Make it into a jQuery object...
        var tweet = $(strHtml);

        // ...so we can append it to our list.
        $list.append(tweet);

        // Store the JSON data for this tweet
        $list.find("a:last").data("tweetJSON", JSON.stringify(data.results[i]));
      }

      // Call the listview widget.
      $list.listview();
```

```
    // Now that it's all done, hide the page loading dialog
    $.mobile.pageLoading(true);

    // When the user taps on a tweet, it will go to the detail page.
    $list.find("a").click(function() {
      var $this = $(this);
      // Pass the tweetJSON object over to the detail page so that it
      // has the information it needs
      $("#pageTweetDetail").data("tweetJSON", $this.data("tweetJSON"));
    })
  },
  error: function() {

    // Get the page
    var $page = $("#pageError .content");

    // Build an error message
    var strHtml = "<h3>Update failed</h3>";
    strHtml += "<p>We were unable to update the twitter feed.
    Please try again.</p>"

    // append it to the error dialog
    $page.html(strHtml);

    // Show the dialog
    $("#show-error-page").click();

    // Hide the page loading dialog
    $.mobile.pageLoading(true);
  }
});
}
```

Now, whenever the application updates the feed, it will display the page loading message. This gives the user visual feedback that the application is doing something, rather than just being arbitrarily frozen. This is an important technique, as users don't mind waiting for applications as long as they know that something's happening.

Finally, if the user enters an invalid Twitter user name on the settings page, the Twitter API will return no results, and right now that just results in a blank list view page. We should display a dialog message to let the user know that they've entered an invalid Twitter user name.

A simple change to the updateTwitterFeed function will handle this (Example 6-9).

Example 6-9. Adding error handling to the updateTwitterFeed function

```
[. . .]

  // Get the tweets and append them to the list
  $.ajax({
    url: strUrl,
    dataType: 'json',
    success: function(data) {
```

```
// Delete the existing list, if any
$page.find(".content").empty();

// Are there even any tweets to display?
if (data.results.length === 0) {

    // display an error message in the error dialog
    var strHtml = "<h3>No Tweets Found</h3>";
    strHtml += "<p>No tweets found for the Twitter user name ";
    strHtml += $page.data("twitterUser") + ".</p>";
    $("#pageError .content").html(strHtml);
    $("#show-error-page").click();

    // Update the list page to reflect that no tweets were found
    $page.find(".content").html("<h3>No Tweets Found</h3>");

    // Hide the page loading dialog
    $.mobile.pageLoading(true);

    // and we're done.
    return;
}
```

[. . .]

Here we are using the error dialog page we set up earlier. So now the application looks as shown in Figure 6-7.

Figure 6-7. jqmTweet: Improved list view

If the user enters a new Twitter user name to search for, the app will show a loading dialog (Figure 6-8).

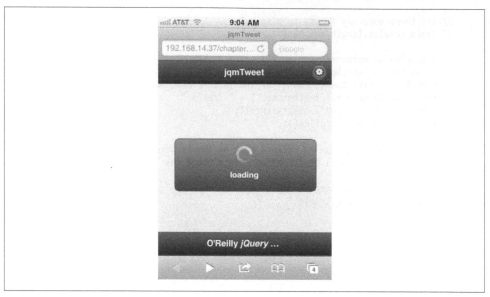

Figure 6-8. jqmTweet: Loading dialog

And if the user enters an invalid Twitter user name to search for, the app will display the error pop up Figure 6-9.

Figure 6-9. jqmTweet: Error pop up

There are plenty of other improvements for jqmTweet: allowing the user to make tweets and handling conversations are the first two features that come to mind. But this basic application demonstrates how to build a jQuery Mobile application.

Overall Approach

In summary, our approach for developing the app was simple:

1. Create simple pages to mock out the application, essentially producing a prototype
2. "Hook up" the pages to the data sources
3. Iterate: improve the results, add features, and fix bugs

This approach works well for jQuery Mobile applications, particularly applications that will use RESTful services. It leverages the speed of jQuery Mobile and scales well to large projects with many participants. It also works well with Agile projects, especially when design and development are proceeding concurrently. It is helpful to have design working at least one sprint ahead of development, but even if it isn't, you can still produce mocked-out pages and style them later as the designs are finalized.

I've found that using jQuery Mobile allows me to produce mobile web applications with amazing speed, especially if you use the framework's strengths. As jQuery Mobile matures, it will undoubtedly include more features and support more devices, allowing us to make awesome applications quickly and easily.

About the Author

Jon Reid is a senior developer at EffectiveUI. He has been developing in HTML and JavaScript since 1996, and is committed to building rich and accessible web experiences. He is passionate about user-centered creative processes and believes that involving the user is an essential part of creating awesome software. Jon has a variety of experience with HTML-based RIAs and has been the lead on projects ranging from genetic analysis software to Microsoft's "I'm a PC" campaign.

Jon is an alumnus of the University of Colorado, Boulder, where he graduated with a degree in Physics and Mathematics. He lives in Denver with his partner of thirteen years.

Colophon

The animal on the cover of *jQuery Mobile*, first edition, is a squirrel tree toad.

The cover image is from *Johnson's Natural History*. The cover font is Adobe ITC Garamond. The text font is Linotype Birka; the heading font is Adobe Myriad Condensed; and the code font is LucasFont's TheSansMonoCondensed.

Have it your way.

Get even more for your money.

Join the O'Reilly Community, and register the O'Reilly books you own. It's free, and you'll get:

- $4.99 ebook upgrade offer
- 40% upgrade offer on O'Reilly print books
- Membership discounts on books and events
- Free lifetime updates to ebooks and videos
- Multiple ebook formats, DRM FREE
- Participation in the O'Reilly community
- Newsletters
- Account management
- 100% Satisfaction Guarantee

Signing up is easy:

1. **Go to: oreilly.com/go/register**
2. **Create an O'Reilly login.**
3. **Provide your address.**
4. **Register your books.**

Note: English-language books only

To order books online:

oreilly.com/store

For questions about products or an order:

orders@oreilly.com

To sign up to get topic-specific email announcements and/or news about upcoming books, conferences, special offers, and new technologies:

elists@oreilly.com

For technical questions about book content:

booktech@oreilly.com

To submit new book proposals to our editors:

proposals@oreilly.com

O'Reilly books are available in multiple DRM-free ebook formats. For more information:

oreilly.com/ebooks

O'REILLY®

Spreading the knowledge of innovators   oreilly.com